Praise for Perry Watts

Perry Watts is a 'master of art' in creative use of SAS/GRAPH® software for informative data displays, and proves that once again in her short book, *Multiple-Plot Displays: Simplified with Macros*. This book is a useful reference with a collection of macro tools for the intermediate-to-advanced SAS/GRAPH user who wishes to learn how to automate the creation of effective, multi-panel graphical displays of possibly complex data or for group-by-group comparisons. In addition, we find some useful tips for using ODS and Web-based drill-down capabilities in multi-panel displays.

Michael Friendly
Author of *Visualizing Categorical Data*
and *SAS® System for Statistical Graphics*

Among the more exacting tasks in SAS/GRAPH® is creating, managing, and replaying multiple graphs. Perry has developed a set of macros that systematize this process. These macros manage the graphics catalogs for you, standardize your plots, format template(s), and then replay your plots through the template(s). Where your plots cannot be entirely standardized, an alternate approach using the Annotate facility is offered. Also included are expositions of SAS/GRAPH output to ODS and philosophies of data visualization, along with an approach to implementing these.

John Cohen
PhilaSUG

SAS Publishing

Multiple-Plot Displays:
Simplified with Macros

Perry Watts

The Power to Know

The correct bibliographic citation for this manual is as follows: Watts, Perry. 2002. *Multiple-Plot Displays: Simplified with Macros.* Cary, NC: SAS Institute Inc.

Multiple-Plot Displays: Simplified with Macros

Table of Contents

Preface

One of the major strengths of SAS/GRAPH software is its facility for generating data-driven graphs. Comparisons can be made easily when multiple plots with a uniform style are sized to fit neatly on a single page. Despite this unique facility, no comprehensive publication exists that takes you from single- to multiple-plot displays while providing the means for simplifying the process along the way. Making the transition with as much ease as is possible is the goal of this book.

I wrote the four extension macros to automate the construction of multiple-plot displays so that you can easily reconstruct graphs until you get what you want. All are available through SAS Online Samples (see inside front cover for details). Here is what they do:

%DELGCAT   deletes all entries in a graphics catalog so that revised graphs can be viewed as intended.

%TMPLT   the flagship macro, creates a template with panels from values assigned to the macro parameters. Underlying panel coordinates are calculated from the parameters so that you can determine where the plots appear on a graph. No longer is it necessary to manually re-calculate panel coordinates.

%TREPLAY   replays plots through the newly-created panels. This macro is contained within %TMPLT.

%SIZEIT   uses some of the parameter values from %TMPLT to correct text and shape distortion that occurs when graphs are displayed through panels that do not conform to the default aspect ratio for a given graphics device.

While the extension macros in this book insulate you from PROC GREPLAY, the procedure is still described in some detail so that you can see how macros actually work. Macro limitations are also cited along with techniques and principles for enhancing multiple-plot displays. In addition, separate sections are devoted to explaining how to work with the Output Delivery System (ODS) and how to develop drill-down graphs on the Web. Given the tools, topics, and concepts described in this book, you should come away with the skills and foundation needed for creating informative, visually appealing multiple-plot displays.

Acknowledgments

I would like to express my appreciation to Patsy Poole of the Books by Users Program and to Art Carpenter, Series Editor, for coordinating this book. I also thank the following SAS employees, who handled editing, production, design, and marketing: Candy Farrell, Beth Heinig, Brad Kellam, Monica McClain, Patricia Spain, and Ericka Wilcher. Valuable technical reviews were performed by Harriet Adams, Melisa Norman, Chris Noto, Jim Sheedy, and Dawn Schrader. In addition, I want to extend a special thanks to John Cohen for suggesting the topic to me as a NESUG '98 presentation as well as to Jan Buzydlowski, Jerry Kagan, and Michael Friendly for their informative reviews of the manuscript. Rudi Bao, a research physician from the Fox Chase Cancer Center, also graciously allowed me to use his mouse tumor growth data displayed in the 16-plot examples, and Dawn Schrader from SAS Technical Support answered my Web/ODS questions about the mouse plots. I also want to acknowledge my manager, Suzanne M. Clark from IMS Health, who encouraged me to write this book by adjusting task assignments for a demanding project.

I am especially grateful to my husband, Samuel Litwin, for his constant support, and for giving me interesting graphics problems to solve when we worked together at Fox Chase.

Using This Book

This book is intended for the experienced SAS/GRAPH user who wants to create multiple-plot displays with tools that partially automate the process. To get the most out of the book, the reader should also have a basic understanding of how the macro language works.

The first chapter sets the stage by defining key graphics elements and by describing when multiple-plot displays should be used in data analysis. The data sources used in this book are also described.

Chapter 2 limits the discussion about the GREPLAY procedure to what is needed for working with the extension macros. Program statements with the NOFS (no full-screen) option are favored over an interactive approach for obtaining graphics output.

Chapter 3 describes the macros and shows how they work in concert to build graphs that are fully legible and pleasing to the eye. Diagrams and plots are used as an aid to clarify points being made. Macro limitations are also discussed.

In Chapter 4 the emphasis switches from the GREPLAY extension macros to their calling programs to promote visual thinning for non-cluttered graphs. Examples of visual thinning are presented along with a small amount of the related code from the calling program's macro. Lengthy code listings are replaced by an outline that lists the functions of a calling program and with a description of the role that the Annotate facility plays in generating customized graphs.

Chapter 5 ties everything together by showing how to construct the survival plots from Chapter 1. SAS code citations are linked to the outline for the calling program from Chapter 4. The survival plots are reviewed because the data are obtained through the Output Delivery System (ODS). Chapter 5 also features two other applications of ODS with drill-down graphs containing hot zones for retrieving enlargements of selected plots.

This book adheres to the format established by Art Carpenter in *Annotate: Simply the Basics* by defining "See Also" sections for relevant information within the book and "More Information" sections for additional articles of interest. All sources are fully cited in the "References" section.

Because the pages in this book are small, abbreviated graphs with fewer plots are used in the chapters as examples. Full-sized graphs with the original number of plots can be found on separate pages in the Appendix.

CHAPTER 1

Introduction to Multiple-Plot Displays

1.1 Definition of Terms

Templates in SAS/GRAPH contain *panels* that define standard shapes, but none of these shapes are curved like the white spaces pictured in the flowchart template above. All panels in a SAS/GRAPH template are measured as percentages of the graphics output area. Panels can rest invisibly on top of each other. Think of a template as a collection of transparent, layered panels through which plots are displayed.

While the relationship between a template and its member panels is readily understood, the first three rows in Table 1.1 show there is no agreement among the experts about how to define the elements of a multiple-plot display. Therefore, the term *graph* is being used in this book to reference a collection of *plots*, and a *plot* is defined more broadly as the singular output from any SAS/GRAPH procedure except GREPLAY. Thus, output from GCHART, GPLOT, and GSLIDE are all defined as *plots* in the book, whereas output from PROC GREPLAY is excluded because it is a *template graph* of multiple plots.

Source	Single Display	Multiple Display
Tukey, John and Paul	Plot	Multiwindow Plot
Tufte	Graphic	Small Multiples
SAS/GRAPH	GRSEG	GRSEG
This book	Plot	Graph

Table 1.1. *In this book single- and multiple-plot displays are defined as plots and graphs, respectively.*

Plots are displayed in the order in which they are created through panels separately ordered by panel number. The position of curves on a plot is determined by the axes definitions within a procedure and not by the values of the underlying panel coordinates.

The macros in this book always reserve the first panel in the upper-left corner for the first plot created in a program, whereas the penultimate panel in the lower-right corner gets the last plot in a series of plots. The last panel in the template covers the entire graphics output area, and it is reserved for the grand title that describes the graph.

Figure 1.1 shows how the graphics elements just described are related to each other. While a graph is simply a page of plots, no clearly defined relationship exists between *plot* and *panel*. Instead, the title panel spans the graphics output area, covering all the other panels in the display, and it is possible for some panels not to be filled with plots when TREPLAY is invoked. Figure 1.1 also shows that it is not necessary for the rows in a graph to contain the same number of panels. Panels are created center-justified by default to compensate for any inequality in row totals. Technically, therefore, the sole panel in the first row of this diagram is defined as the first panel in the upper-left corner of the graph.

A few additional graphics elements are also depicted in Figure 1.1. A *margin* of an arbitrary size can be placed around the small plots in the graph, and each of the small plots can be *scaled* to a factor less than 1.0. Scaling separates panels so that plots stand out better. In effect, it defines an additional margin around each individual panel.

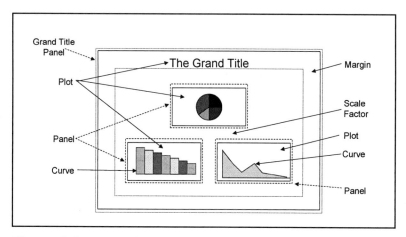

Figure 1.1 *Schematic of a graph showing the relationship of plots to panel displays. The four extension macros in this book take the drudgery out of creating panels through which plots are displayed. Any time the margin or the scale factor is changed in a graph, all panel coordinates have to be recalculated. This translates to 32 coordinates for the schematic above because each of the four panels has eight coordinates.*

More Information

For creative uses of template designs, see
Brown, 1991.
Carpenter and Shipp, 1995, Section 6.3, "Controlling Graphical Displays with Templates," pp. 154–184.
Kalt, 1986.
Kirk and Horney, 1998.

For a depiction of the graphical output area, see Carpenter, 1999, p. 17.

For definitions of terms abstracted from their context, see
Tufte, 1983, pp. 14–15 and 170.
Tukey, J., 1977, p. 129.
Tukey, P. and J., 1981, pp. 231–232.

1.2 When Multiple-Plot Displays are Needed

When data contain many subpopulations that cannot be summarized by a single statistic, multiple-plot displays are the graph of choice for visual by-group comparisons.

The example that proves this assertion is taken from Appendix I of Kalbfleisch and Prentice (1980) and reproduced in *SAS/STAT User's Guide, Version 8*, Example 37.1 for the LIFETEST procedure (p.1832). Figure 1.2a is an enhanced reproduction of the graph that appears on page 1840 of *SAS/STAT User's Guide, Version 8*. If you work in the pharmaceutical industry, you will recognize the survival plot in Figure 1.2a as a primary vehicle for communicating information about a Phase III clinical trial.

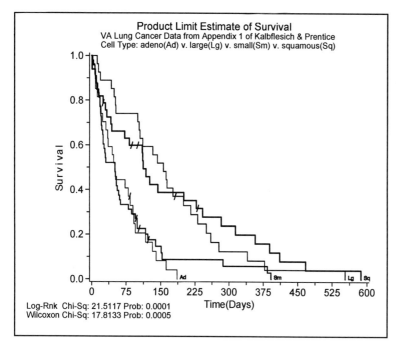

Figure 1.2a *Reproduction of Output 37.1.6: Graph of the Estimated Survival rates annotated with log-rank and Wilcoxon chi-square statistics, showing statistically significant results that can be attributed to the presence of non-overlapping strata.*

Visually, you can corroborate the significance of a chi-square statistic by looking for strata (curves) that are non-overlapping. In this case, the paired Adeno|Small and Large|Squamous strata are responsible for the statistically significant results (prob<0.05). The four strata are also spread far enough apart so that they can be fully tracked.

The situation becomes much more challenging when the reviewer wants to know if treatment affects survival. Figure 1.2b displays eight strata: two for each cell type/treatment combination. Again, the log-rank and Wilcoxon chi-square tests are statistically significant, but you would be hard-pressed to find all pairs of non-overlapping strata that contribute to the significant result. Also, Cell Type probably should be held constant before comparing treatment regimens. Figure 1.2c does this with an abbreviated display of two plots for the Large and Squamous Cell Types. Results for these more meaningful comparisons are insignificant.

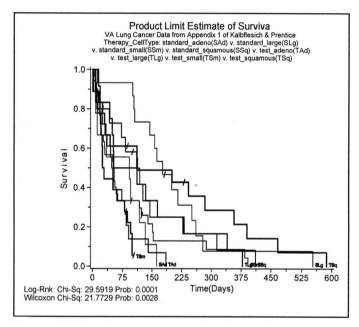

Figure 1.2b *All combinations of cell and treatment types appear in separate strata in one plot producing an unreadable graph of questionable value. There is no way to identify the non-overlapping strata that would contribute to a significant result.*

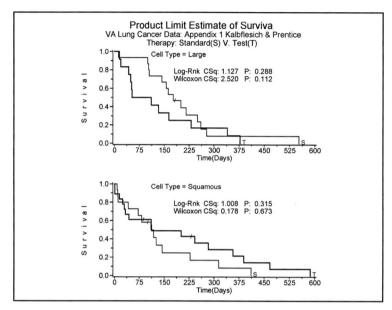

Figure 1.2c *The effect of treatment is clearly discernable in a multiple-plot display that compares two strata at a time. Results are not significant because the strata overlap. Additional two-strata graphs can be found in the Appendix.*

1.3 Data Sources Used in This Book Require Multiple-Plot Displays

Each of the data sources in this book is described in this section. Each description enumerates the subpopulations in the data that require their own separate plot.

Survival Data (see Chapters 1 and 5)

As mentioned, the survival data are taken from Appendix I of Kalbfleish and Prentice (1980). They have been used to demonstrate an application of the LIFETEST procedure in Versions 6 and 8 of the *SAS/STAT User's Guide*. The response variable is survival time, and it is measured in days for a lung cancer patient. Censored events occur when no follow-up information is available for a patient who leaves the study prematurely. Censors are denoted by a forward slash (/) on the graphs. Additional covariates in the data besides *Cell Type* and *Therapy* are *Prior Therapy, Age, Diagnosis Time,* and *Performance Status* (*SAS/STAT User's Guide, Version 8,* p. 1831).

Mouse Tumor Data (see Chapters 2 through 5)

The mouse tumor data come from a research study conducted by Dr. Rudi Bao of the Fox Chase Cancer Center in Philadelphia, Pennsylvania. Four treatment regimens are applied to right and left flank tumors of a group of 32 mice. Tumor measurements taken at unequal time intervals are plotted as cubic regression curves for each mouse.

Format Optimization Study (see Chapter 4)

Format resolution times are recorded for different distributions of start values created by serial applications of the SAS RANUNI function. The start values in each distribution are sorted by frequency and then renamed to reflect their sort order (e.g., a start value of '1' also has the highest frequency). Because start values are renamed, binary, sequential, and embedded formats can be ranked by their resolution times.

Baseball Data (see Chapters 4 and 5)

The scatterplot matrix in Michael Friendly's *SAS System for Statistical Graphics* is redrafted as an upper triangular matrix to eliminate redundant transpositions and to demonstrate the flexibility of the TMPLT macro. The data set "contains variables that measure batting and fielding performance for 322 regular and substitute hitters in the 1986 year, their career performance statistics, and their salary at the start of the 1987 season" (Friendly, p. 598).

Shannon Scores for Amino Acid Diversity (see Chapter 3)

Cumulative distributions of Shannon scores (H) ± 1 standard deviations for numbered sites in replicates of the VAlpha, VBeta, and VKappa genes are displayed along with a schematic graph that shows how they are mapped to a gene backbone containing X,Y, and Z coordinates.

A review of the data dimensions for the graphs demonstrates that they are ideal candidates for multiple-plot displays. None of their subpopulations can be summarized by one statistic:

Survival Data: Each cell type contains two treatment regimens. Each treatment is a stratum in a survival plot.

Mouse Tumor Data: Each treatment group contains multiple mice. Each mouse has right and left tumor measurements that are plotted over time.

Format Optimization Study: Each format search type is tested with a different frequency distribution of start values. Each distribution is plotted with a step function.

Baseball Data: Each combination of variables generates a plot. Each plot is a scatter plot of discrete points.

Shannon Scores: Each graph contains multiple genes. Each gene contains many sites with Shannon scores.

See Also

Chapters 4 and 5 contain detailed descriptions of selected graphs.

Enlargements of some of the graphs can be found in the Appendix.

More Information

For a discussion of the role of graphics in data analysis, see Friendly, 1991, Chapter 1.

For a description of the baseball data, see Friendly, 1991, pp. 13–14, 577–581, and 598–607.

For a description of the Shannon scores, see Watts and Litwin, 1992.

For a description of the format optimization study, see Watts, 2001, "On the Relationship between Format Structure and Efficiency in SAS."

CHAPTER 2

Working with GREPLAY

The interplay among graphics catalog types, along with the flexibility of the GREPLAY procedure itself, make it difficult to come up with the right order in which to present the topics that are covered in this chapter. Therefore, a somewhat arbitrary decision has been made to start with the catalog, and then proceed to the syntax, definitions, usage, and catalog entry management. A final section that describes how the graphic elements in the GREPLAY procedure relate to each other can be skipped over without sacrificing continuity. However, if you want to understand the TMPLT macro better, you should not bypass it.

2.1 The Role of the Catalog in Graphics Generation

Catalogs play an integral role in the GREPLAY procedure. As Figure 2.1 demonstrates, output from all SAS/GRAPH procedures is stored in a catalog. This fact may not be so apparent, since default assignments are made in the absence of explicit definitions. For example, the following two statements are identical:

```
proc gslide;
run;

proc gslide gout=work.gseg;
run;
```

While most of the catalog management occurs inside PROC GREPLAY, the GOUT, NAME, and DESCRIPTION options are attached to other SAS/GRAPH procedures to capture graphics output as it is generated. GOUT names the graphics output catalog whereas NAME and DESCRIPTION identify the plots or entries that make up the catalog. In contrast to graphics catalog options, template catalog references and the IGOUT statement for input graphics catalogs are confined to PROC GREPLAY.

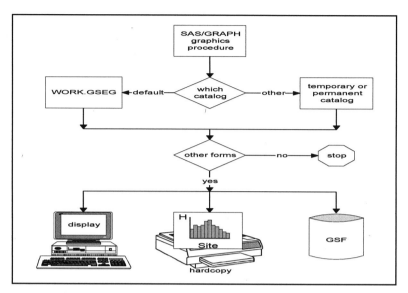

Figure 2.1   *This reproduction of Figure 44.1 in SAS/GRAPH Software Usage, Version 6 shows how graphics output is produced.*

2.2 GREPLAY Syntax

PROC GREPLAY is difficult to understand partly because of its flexibility. An examination of the syntax shows that there are no mandatory statement options!

```
 PROC GREPLAY <BYLINE>
<CC=color-map-catalog>
<CMAP=color-map-entry>
<FS>
<GOUT=<libref.>output-catalog>
<IGOUT=<libref.>input-catalog>
<IMAGEMAP=output-data-set>
<NOBYLINE>
<NOFS>
<PRESENTATION>
<TC=template-catalog>
<TEMPLATE=template-entry>;
```

In addition, each statement option in PROC GREPLAY can be executed separately as a single statement. For example, GREPLAY only needs to be invoked once to switch from NOFS for line-mode interaction to FS with windows display:

```
proc greplay nofs;
   fs;
run;
```

Because of the flexibility, a single listing of the procedure syntax is not very informative. Which catalog is needed depends upon the task that is being undertaken. For example a template catalog (TC) has to be specified if a template is being defined with TDEF. Graphics output only can be COPIED from an input (IGOUT) catalog to an output (GOUT) catalog, and if a plot is being TREPLAYed through a template panel, then both the graphics catalog (IGOUT) and the template catalog (TC) have to be specified. Given the possibility of so many scenarios, relevant procedure syntax will be presented alongside code examples as they are reviewed in this chapter.

See Also

See Table 1.1 in Chapter 1 for a definition of terms. This book differentiates between single- and multiple-plot displays by defining them as *plots* and *graphs,* respectively. A graph built from the TMPLT macro is an aggregate type with a one-to-one relationship to its supporting template and graphics catalogs. Please see the entity-relationship diagram in Section 2.6 for a pictorial representation of this relationship.

More Information

For code examples of the GOUT, NAME, and DESCRIPTION options attached to an application of GCHART, see Miron, 1995, pp. 259–264.

The GREPLAY procedure syntax is listed on pages 924–925 in *SAS/GRAPH Software: Reference, for Version 8, Volume 2.*

2.3 GREPLAY Definitions

It is necessary to use the GREPLAY procedure to reproduce plots that have been stored as entries in a graphics catalog. More specifically, GREPLAY enables you to

- select entries for REPLAY or TREPLAY

- design templates for TREPLAY

- manage entries in the graphics, template, or color map catalogs.

Replay sends output directly to the screen or printer whereas TREPLAY for template-replay replays one or more plots through an intervening template onto the screen or printer. REPLAY is not discussed further because it plays no role in the creation of a multiple-plot display.

Tables 2.3a–2.3c summarize GREPLAY features used throughout this book. The summary is drawn from Chapter 36, "The GREPLAY Procedure," in *SAS/GRAPH Software: Reference, Version 6*. The features described for GREPLAY in this chapter work as expected in all releases of Version 8 SAS software. Please note that the extension macros described in this book may or may not be listed with a % sign. For example, the terms "TMPLT macro" and "%TMPLT" referenced in Figure 2.3b are synonymous.

GREPLAY Option	Description
IGOUT	Specifies the name of the input graphics catalog. There is no default.
GOUT	Specifies the output graphics catalog. The default is WORK.GSEG.
NOFS	Specifies the use of line-mode rather than full-screen mode.
TC	Specifies the name of the template catalog to use with GREPLAY. There is no default.
TEMPLATE	Identifies a template entry by name within the template catalog (TC). There is no default.

Table 2.3a *These GREPLAY options are used in the macros or in the graphics programs that invoke them. The NOFS, TC, and TEMPLATE options are confined to the extension macros.*

GREPLAY Statement	Description
COPY	Copies GRSEG entries from the IGOUT catalog to the GOUT catalog.
DELETE	Deletes GRSEG entries from the IGOUT catalog.
LIST	Writes entries from input and template catalogs to the SAS LOG.
TDEF	Defines or modifies the panels of a template in the current template catalog. Options associated with TDEF can be found in Table 2.3c.
TREPLAY	Uses the following syntax to select a plot for display through a panel: panel#:entry-ID or entry# The panel# is associated with a panel in the named template, and entry-ID identifies a plot in an IGOUT graphics catalog. See Figures 2.4.1a and 2.4.2 for examples.

Table 2.3b *These GREPLAY statements are applied to the IGOUT catalog. TDEF is used for creating a new template in %TMPLT. TREPLAY is used in open code or in the TREPLAY macro. See Section 3.4 for additional details.*

TDEF Option	Description
CLIP	Output from background panels is not visible. Recall from Chapter 1 that panels can be layered.
COLOR	Specifies the panel border color. Otherwise no border is displayed.
LLX LLY LRX LRY ULX ULY URX URY	Specifies eight X and Y coordinates in a panel: (ULX, ULY) (URX, URY) (LLX, LLY) (LRX, LRY) U or L in the first character position references U(pper) and L(ower). L or R in the second position references L(eft) and R(ight). X or Y in the third character position references horizontal and vertical directions, respectively.
ROTATE	Specifies the rotation angle of a panel in degrees.
SCALEX SCALEY	Panels can be scaled independently in the X or Y direction. (1=no scale; <1 decreases the panel size, thereby increasing the amount of space around a panel; >1 increases panel size). %TMPLT does not accommodate values greater than 1.
XLATEX XLATEY	Specifies the distance to move a panel in the X or Y direction.

Table 2.3c   *TDEF options operate on individual panels in a template. %TMPLT uses all of the options.*

More Information

For articles that summarize features of the GREPLAY procedure see
    Carpenter and Shipp, 1995
    Gilbert, 2000
    Jacobs, 1993
    Mitchell, 1992
    Rooth, 1987
    SAS/GRAPH Software: Usage, Version 6, Part 9, pp. 589–664
    Watts, 1998

Carpenter and Shipp, 1995, provide an interesting example of the CLIP option, p. 179, demonstrating that foreground panels become opaque when background panels are clipped.

Jacobs, 1993, recommends panel rotation when a switch is made from landscape to portrait mode.

2.4 GREPLAY: Usage

2.4.1 Working with existing catalogs

<table>
<tr><td align="center">*Syntax*</td><td align="center">*Example*</td></tr>
<tr><td></td><td>

```
proc greplay
  nofs
  igout = MyLib.GrfCat
  tc = MyLib.TmpCat
  template = T1X2;
  treplay 1:GPLOT
          2:GPLOT1
          3:GPLOT2
          4:GSLIDE;
run;
```

</td></tr>
</table>

PROC GREPLAY

<NOFS>

<IGOUT = *input-catalog*>

<TC = *template-catalog*>

<TEMPLATE = *template-name*>;

<TREPLAY *panel#:entry-id*>;

Figure 2.4.1a *Syntax and example of the GREPLAY procedure used for generating a graph from existing template and graphics catalogs. The left arrow links the panel coordinates stored in* **MyLib.TmpCat.T1X2** *to the panel numbers in the treplay command. Similarly, the right arrow points to the plots from the graphics catalog,* **MyLib.GrfCat**, *which are displayed through the panels.*

The catalog entry type for the input graphics catalog (IGOUT) is a *plot* or GRSEG whereas it is a *template* in the template catalog. The template contains X and Y coordinates for each member panel as well as values for the other TDEF options listed in Table 2.3c.

While it is possible to store plots for many graphs in a single permanent graphics catalog, this practice increases the difficulty of catalog management for multiple-plot displays. Unlike the template catalog (TC) that maintains a fixed relationship between a member template and a panel within the template, there is no SAS option that links an IGOUT catalog entry to a specific graph containing a predefined set of plots.

One of the underlying assumptions in this book, therefore, is that a separate graphics catalog is created for each graph with member entries being generated for the plots as described in Chapter 1. This way, the *entry-name* in the TREPLAY (template-replay) command can be replaced by the easier-to-manage *Entry-ID#* for positioning plots on a page. In other words, replace

$$\text{panel\#:}\textit{entry-name} \qquad (1\text{:GCHART1})$$

with

$$\text{panel\#:}\textit{entry-ID\#} \qquad (1\text{:}1)$$

where the second number after the colon reflects a plot's order of creation. All you have to do then is to create the plots in a top-down, left-to-right order to get the desired output from %TMPLT and %TREPLAY. Catalog entries are always stored in the order in which they are created.

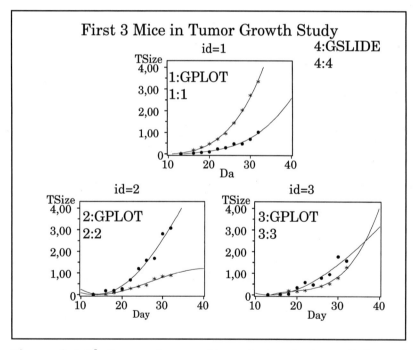

Figure 2.4.1b *Four panels are on this graph: three for the small plots and one for the grand title that covers the entire graphics output region. TREPLAY commands are superimposed on the corresponding plots.*

2.4.2 Defining and using a new template in GREPLAY

Both the TDEF and TEMPLATE statements are needed for creating new templates in GREPLAY. TDEF is used for creation, and the TEMPLATE statement tells GREPLAY to use the newly created template to create the output. The TMPLT macro automates TDEF, so that it is no longer necessary to calculate panel coordinates by hand. Additional panel options XLATEX, XLATEY, SCALEX, SCALEY, CLIP, BORDER, and ROTATE referenced in the syntax section of Figure 2.4.2 become template options in the macro because the same value for a given option is assigned to every panel in the template except the grand title panel. Identical values for these options cause panels to be repositioned as a unit. This point needs to be emphasized, for it is the key to the macro's versatility.

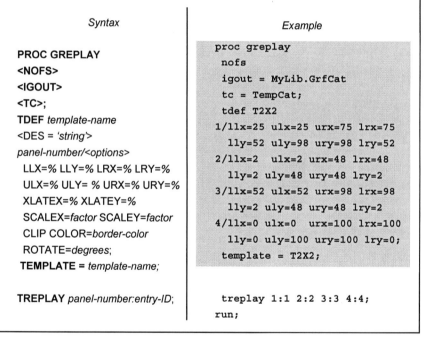

Syntax	*Example*
PROC GREPLAY	`proc greplay`
<NOFS>	` nofs`
<IGOUT>	` igout = MyLib.GrfCat`
<TC>;	` tc = TempCat;`
TDEF *template-name*	` tdef T2X2`
<DES = '*string***'>**	`1/llx=25 ulx=25 urx=75 lrx=75`
panel-number/**<***options***>**	`   lly=52 uly=98 ury=98 lry=52`
LLX=% LLY=% LRX=% LRY=%	`2/llx=2  ulx=2 urx=48 lrx=48`
ULX=% ULY= % URX=% URY=%	`   lly=2 uly=48 ury=48 lry=2`
XLATEX=% XLATEY=%	`3/llx=52 ulx=52 urx=98 lrx=98`
SCALEX=*factor* SCALEY=*factor*	`   lly=2 uly=48 ury=48 lry=2`
CLIP COLOR=*border-color*	`4/llx=0 ulx=0  urx=100 lrx=100`
ROTATE=*degrees*;	`   lly=0 uly=100 ury=100 lry=0;`
TEMPLATE = *template-name;*	`template = T2X2;`
TREPLAY *panel-number:entry-ID;*	` treplay 1:1 2:2 3:3 4:4;`
	`run;`

Figure 2.4.2   *The template for Figure 2.3.1b is created from scratch in PROC GREPLAY. The four panels defined with a TDEF statement reference coordinate units that are percentages of the graphics output area. The TREPLAY command is then issued to display four plots from **MyLib.GrfCat** through the newly defined panels. The plots are displayed in the order in which they were created.*

Actions for the shaded area in Figure 2.4.2 are taken over by the TMPLT macro, and the treplay command is handled by %TREPLAY contained within %TMPLT.

2.5 Managing Entries in the Graphics and Template Catalogs

GREPLAY is used for managing catalogs. Common tasks that require the management capabilities of PROC GREPLAY are listed below. While an extension macro also can be used to delete catalog entries, the remaining tasks are completed on an as-needed basis in open code.

To delete all the entries in the default graphics catalog:

```
proc greplay igout=WORK.GSEG nofs;
   delete _all_;
run;
```

Graphics catalog entries cannot be overwritten. Instead, they must first be deleted and then re-created. %DELGCAT performs this task. Template catalog entries, on the other hand, can be overwritten. A new version of the default template, TMPMAC, is automatically re-created when %TMPLT is invoked without a parameter value for TNAME (template-name). Note that a TDELETE statement is available for removing templates from template catalogs.

To list entries in a graphics catalog:

```
proc greplay igout=MYLIB.GRFCAT nofs;
   list igout;
run;
```

The following output written to the SAS LOG references plots displayed in Figure 2.4.1b:

```
NOTE: Graphs on MYLIB.GRFCAT
      NAME              DESCRIPTION
   ----------        ----------------------------
   1  GPLOT        I   Plot of LeftT * day
                       id=1
   2  GPLOT1       I   Plot of LeftT * day
                       id=2
   3  GPLOT2       I   Plot of LeftT * day
                       id=3
   4  GSLIDE       I   OUTPUT FROM PROC GSLIDE
   5  TEMPLATE     I   TEMPLATE GRAPH PRODUCED BY
                       GREPLAY
```

To list panels in a template:

```
proc greplay tc=MYLIB.TMPCAT nofs;
  template T1X2;
  list template;
run;
```

The following output written to the SAS LOG lists the panel coordinates for the plots displayed in Figure 2.4.1b:

Pan	Clp	Color	Ll-x	Ll-y	Ul-x	Ul-y	Ur-x	Ur-y	Lr-x	Lr-y
1			25	52	25	98	75	98	75	52
2			2	2	2	48	48	48	48	2
3			52	2	52	48	98	48	98	2
4			0	0	0	100	100	100	100	0

To display a graph with a CC (color catalog) through a template:

Entries from three catalogs have to be properly identified in the following code so that a graph is displayed as intended. An example of the CDEF (color definition) option is supplied, showing that colors can be mapped to hexadecimal numbers representing the RGB (red/green/blue) color scheme.

```
proc greplay cc=WORK.clrmap
             gout=work.gseg nofs;
  cdef mycolor
    1 / black : CX707070  /* dark gray   */
    2 / green : CX9C9C9C  /* medium gray */
    3 / blue  : CXCACACA; /* light gray  */
run;


proc greplay igout=work.gseg
             tc=work.tempcat
             cc=work.clrmap nofs;
  template TmpMac;
  cmap MyColor;
  treplay 1:1 2:2 3:3 4:4;
run;
```

<u>To create a permanent catalog with COPY: (COPY a temporary catalog entry to a permanent catalog)</u>

Use a COPY statement to move entries from one graphics catalog to another. Be forewarned, however, that results can be unpredictable if you are copying entries to a pre-existing target catalog. If GCHART is already in MYLIB.GRFCAT, for example, GCHART1 is written to MYLIB.GRFCAT even when you COPY GCHART as shown below. It is best, therefore, to transfer final versions of plots to target catalogs or to delete all of the entries from the target catalog and COPY afresh.

```
/*Remember IGOUT is the input graphics catalog.
        GOUT is the output graphics catalog. */


    proc greplay igout=work.gseg
                gout=MYLIB.grfcat nofs;
      copy GCHART;
    run;
```

or

```
    proc greplay igout=work.gseg
                gout=MYLIB.grfcat nofs;
      copy _ALL_;
    run;
```

You can attach a GOUT option to most graphics procedures to send GRSEG entries directly to permanent catalogs.

<u>To create a graph containing entries from multiple catalogs: (do the opposite from above; i.e. COPY a permanent catalog entry to a temporary catalog)</u>

To display a copied plot in the correct panel, you must issue the COPY command at the right place in your SAS program. If three entries are already in WORK.GSEG, for example, GCHART copied from pre-existing MYLIB.GRFCAT in the code sample below becomes the fourth. All plots are then displayed with a second call to GREPLAY that changes the argument to IGOUT from MYLIB.GRFCAT to WORK.GSEG. This way, all of the entries from WORK.GSEG, including the one originally from MYLIB.GRFCAT, can be displayed with a TREPLAY statement. It is necessary to COPY to WORK.GSEG because TREPLAY only works with one graphics catalog at a time. The following code creates a single graph from plots stored originally in two catalogs. Figure 2.5 is an annotated display created by this code.

```
*-- plots 1-3 have been created during the current
       session. Their output has been written to WORK.GSEG;

*-- plot #4;
    proc greplay igout=MYLIB.GRFCAT
                 gout=WORK.GSEG nofs;
        COPY gchart;   ❶
    run;

*-- plot #5 directs output to WORK.GSEG;
    proc gslide;
      title1 h=3
      'Format Resolution Times for 1,000 Start Values';
      title2 h=2.75
      'Frequency Distribution: Modal Region(90%) Tail(10%)';
    run;

    proc greplay igout=WORK.GSEG tc=TEMPCAT nofs;   ❷
    TEMPLATE=Tmpmac;
      ...
    run;
      ...
    treplay 1:1 2:2 3:3 4:4 5:5;   ❷
    quit;   ❸
```

❶ GCHART is copied from MYLIB.GRFCAT to WORK.GSEG.

❷ These invocations of PROC GREPLAY and TREPLAY are taken over by the TMPLT macro. The macro automatically displays all entries in a graphics catalog.

❸ Section 2.7 explains the need for a QUIT statement.

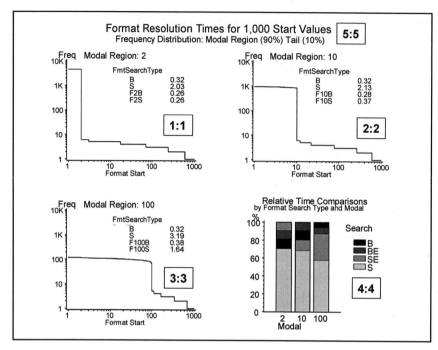

Figure 2.5   *A graph annotated with TREPLAY commands showing plots coming from different catalogs. Plots #1–3 and #5 come from the current run (WORK.GSEG), and plot #4 was created in a prior session.*

More Information
For an example of catalog management in GREPLAY, see Corning, 1994.
For another method of "renaming" graphics catalog entries, see Elkin, 1999.
For a description of the color-naming schemes used in SAS, see *SAS/GRAPH Software: Reference, Version 6*, pp. 182–193.
For an alternative to hard-coding hexadecimal RGB color codes for the CC (color catalogs), see Watts, 2001, *Defining Colors with Precision in your SAS/GRAPH Application*.
For GREPLAY code examples and graphics displays, see http://www.sas.com/techsup/download/sample/graph/greplay-examples-list.html.

2.6 Relationships among Graphics Elements in GREPLAY

The terms "graph" and "plot" were explicitly defined in Chapter 1. While the terms were originally conceived to compensate for a lack of rigor in the field of computer graphics, they also were coined to reflect the relationship among the graphics elements in the GREPLAY procedure when it is invoked from inside the TMPLT macro. The entity-relationship diagram in Figure 2.6 depicts the relationship for GREPLAY in both settings: open code and TMPLT macro. Square brackets for key joins in open code emphasize the flexibility of GREPLAY, a point that was made earlier when procedure syntax was described. In contrast, the more restrictive set of relationships among GREPLAY elements inside the TMPLT macro are depicted with parentheses. Far from being a liability, the restrictions are used to simplify the code for the TMPLT macro. If you can relate to GREPLAY in both open and macro settings, you will make better use of the TMPLT macro in your own applications. Therefore, spend a little extra time on this section and return to it, if needed, after reading the next chapter on the extension macros.

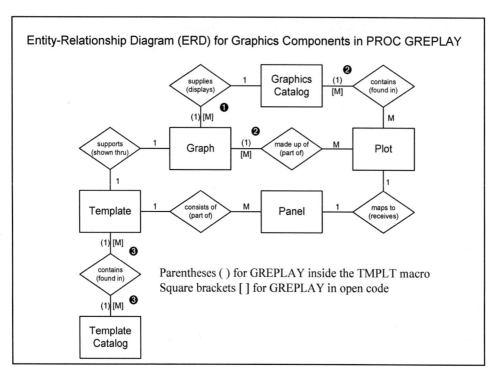

Figure 2.6   *An entity-relationship diagram shows how aggregate catalogs and graphs relate to each other and to their scalar panels and plots. 1 (one) or M (many) represent the maximum number of entities that can be targeted in a join. Joins are always smaller or more restrictive when GREPLAY in the TMPLT macro is different from open code.*

In Figure 2.6 entities or graphics elements are shown in the rectangles, and their relationships are listed in the diamond shapes. To read the diagram, start at a rectangle referencing an entity in the singular and apply the text in the diamond that best describes the bi-directional relationship to get to the next entity. For example:

   A template *consists of* M (many) panels. A panel is *part of* 1 (one) template.

   A template *supports* 1 (one) graph. A graph is *shown through* 1 (one) template.

Joins that are different in the TMPLT macro and open code are discussed next.

❶ TMPLT macro: A graphics catalog supplies (plots) to **one** graph. A graph displays (all) plots from one graphics catalog.

   Open code: A graphics catalog supplies (plots) to **many** graphs . A graph displays plots from one graphics catalog.

The TMPLT macro is more restrictive: a graphics catalog supplies entries to *one and only one graph*, and for the TREPLAY macro to work from inside the TMPLT macro, *all* entries from the graphics catalog are displayed in lockstep order on a graph that can span one or more pages. If you only want a subset of plots from a graphics catalog or if you want to change the order in which the plots appear on a page, disable the TREPLAY macro inside %TMPLT and issue a separate call to TRPELAY in open code. Appropriate references are listed in the "See Also" section.

❷ TMPLT macro: A graphics catalog contains many plots. A plot is found in **one** graphics catalog. A graph is made up of many plots. A plot is part of **one** graph.

   Open code: A graphics catalog contains many plots. A plot is found in **many** graphics catalogs. A graph is made up of many plots. A Plot is part of **many** graphs.

The COPY command described in Section 2.5 has to be used in open code because it places the same entry or plot into many graphics catalogs. Nevertheless, you still can generate differenct looking graphs with the same graphics catalog simply by issuing the TMPLT macro multiple times with different parameter values.

❸ TMPLT macro: A template is found in **one** template catalog. A template catalog contains **one** template.

   Open code: A template is found in **many** template catalogs. A template catalog contains **many** templates.

Ordinarily, a single template can be stored in many catalogs, and a catalog contains many templates. However, templates are re-created every time the TMPLT macro is run, and typically they are stored in their own separate WORK catalogs. This way the most complex many-to-many join is converted to its simplest form—the one-to-one join. While this structure is more rigid, it is also simpler and makes automation possible. In addition, you don't end up with a plethora of catalogs because they are deleted or overwritten between macro executions.

A second look at the large number of entities and relationships in the entity-relationship diagram in Figure 2.6 underscores the complexity of the GREPLAY procedure. And the diagram is not even complete! No accomodations have been made for CC, CMAP or IMAGEMAP entities. Small wonder then that a QUIT is required for a complete exit from GREPLAY. The chapter concludes with a brief description of this command.

See Also

For code examples that compare the use of TREPLAY in open code and TMPLT macro, see the USAGE section in TMPLT.SAS in the Appendix.

For how to create left-justified plots by invoking TREPLAY in open code, see Section 3.5.

The upper triangular matrix of baseball data described in Section 4.4 is also constructed by invoking TREPLAY in open code.

PLOT32MICEHTML.SAS in SAS Online Samples invokes the TMPLT macro twice with the same graphics catalog listed for the GOUT option. Two 16-plot drill-down graphs take the viewer to four-plot enlargements.

More Information

For an informative discussion about the catalog as an aggregate type, see Shoemaker, 2000.

For an introductory text about relational database theory, see McFadden and Hoffer.

2.7 Quitting from PROC GREPLAY

PROC GREPLAY continues to run until it is stopped with QUIT, STOP, or END statements or when the session terminates. The step-boundary RUN statement is not sufficient to terminate GREPLAY. Therefore, it is best to issue a QUIT as the last command in a graphics program that is run iteratively.

CHAPTER 3

The Macros

3.1 Introduction

The four GREPLAY extension macros listed in the Preface are described in this chapter:

%DELGCAT   deletes all entries in a graphics catalog so that revised graphs can be viewed as intended.

%TMPLT   the flagship macro, creates a template from values assigned to the macro parameters.

%TREPLAY   replays plots through the newly created panels. This macro is contained within %TMPLT.

%SIZEIT   uses some of the parameter values from %TMPLT to correct text and shape distortion that occurs when graphs are displayed through panels that do not conform to the default aspect ratio for a given graphics device.

In this chapter, the purpose of each macro is described along with instructions for usage and a code description. Diagrams and graphs are included for clarification. In addition, another solution to the image distortion problem is described when the SIZEIT macro is reviewed. The alternative solution shows that the extension macros do have their limitations.

As mentioned in the introduction, you can use the macros without being proficient in the SAS macro language. Therefore, skipping over the code description sections in this chapter will not disturb continuity. It should be noted, however, that Release 6.12 or later of SAS software is required for the TMPLT and SIZEIT macros, since they use the SYSEVALF macro function for floating-point evaluation.

The chapter concludes with a pseudo-code listing showing the order in which the macros are called. While all the macros except %TREPLAY are functionally independent, they are still designed to work together. Therefore, when different macros reference the same parameters the values for those parameters should be the same.

3.2 %DELGCAT Deletes All Entries in a Graphics Catalog

Purpose

To simulate an over-write operation, graphics catalog entries must first be deleted then re-created. The %DELGCAT macro streamlines the process by deleting all entries in the named IGOUT graphics catalog.

Usage

```
%DELGCAT(work.gseg);
```

deletes all entries in WORK.GSEG.

Code Description

```
%macro DELGCAT(CatName);
  %if %sysfunc(cexist(&CatName)) %then %do;   ❶
    proc greplay igout=&CatName nofs;
      delete _all_;
    run;
  %end;
    quit;
%mend DELGCAT;
```

❶   The CEXIST function ensures that a catalog exists prior to deleting entries from it.

3.3 %TMPLT Creates a Template with Panel Definitions

Purpose

Typically, many revisions are required before a graphics project is completed. As mentioned previously, revisions frequently involve the recalculation of coordinates associated with template panels. Until recently, panel definitions either had to be available as template catalog entries or they had to be manually regenerated. Figure 3.3a shows a typical starting point for a multiple-plot display, and Figure 3.3b points to a significant improvement.

In Figure 3.3a, the title is in the data area. Creating panels in a template that range from 0 to 100% in equal intervals for both coordinate systems leaves no room for a title. Also, the axes values and data points are too small, and the X-axis and by-group labels are too close to each other. In Figure 3.3b, all these problems are fixed.

See Also

See Section 4.2 in Chapter 4 for an enhanced version of Figure 3.3b that removes the inner axes labels from the graph.

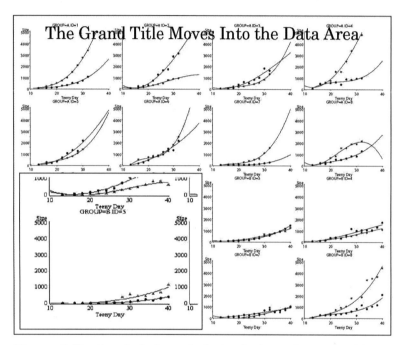

Figure 3.3a *First draft of a multiple-plot display with many problems. The insert is a screen snapshot of one of the small plots.*

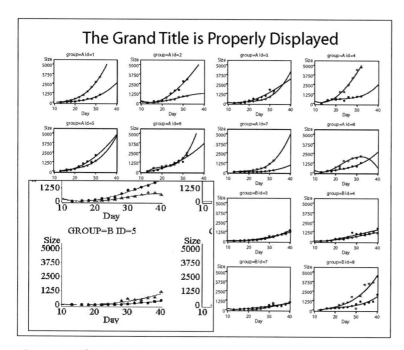

Figure 3.3b *While the plots are smaller than those in Figure 3.3a, the graph is more readable. Again, the insert is a screen snapshot of one of the small plots.*

While Figure 3.3b is more readable, an examination of the panel coordinates in Figure 3.3c shows that the process for template redefinition has to be automated.

Pan	Ll-x	Ll-y	Ul-x	Ul-y	Ur-x	Ur-y	Lr-x	Lr-y
1	5.9	71.4	5.9	92.1	26.6	92.1	26.6	71.4
2	28.4	71.4	28.4	92.1	49.1	92.1	49.1	71.4
3	50.9	71.4	50.9	92.1	71.6	92.1	71.6	71.4
4	73.4	71.4	73.4	92.1	94.1	92.1	94.1	71.4
5	5.9	48.9	5.9	69.6	26.6	69.6	26.6	48.9
6	28.4	48.9	28.4	69.6	49.1	69.6	49.1	48.9
7	50.9	48.9	50.9	69.6	71.6	69.6	71.6	48.9
8	73.4	48.9	73.4	69.6	94.1	69.6	94.1	48.9
9	5.9	26.4	5.9	47.1	26.6	47.1	26.6	26.4
10	28.4	26.4	28.4	47.1	49.1	47.1	49.1	26.4
11	50.9	26.4	50.9	47.1	71.6	47.1	71.6	26.4
12	73.4	26.4	73.4	47.1	94.1	47.1	94.1	26.4
13	5.9	3.9	5.9	24.6	26.6	24.6	26.6	3.9
14	28.4	3.9	28.4	24.6	49.1	24.6	49.1	3.9

Figure 3.3c. *When plots are repositioned on a page, all coordinates have to be recalculated. This amounts to 136 coordinates for the template that supports the graph in Figure 3.3b.*

More Information

For additional articles on automated template definitions, see
   Noto, 1997.
   Westerlund, 1999.
   The PANELS macro in Friendly, 2000.

Usage

To obtain a customized graph such as the one displayed in Figure 3.3b, it is necessary to understand the meaning of the parameters passed to %TMPLT. The most important fact to remember is that values for panel definition parameters are applied uniformly to the small panels in the newly created template. Again, that is how the macro transforms *panel* characteristics into *template* definitions. The grand title panel is always created inside the macro as the last panel in the template. It requires no parameter values for its creation.

Parameter Definitions for %TMPLT		
Parameter	**Description and Range**	**Default**
Margin Parameter		
MARGIN	The group of small, equal-sized panels can have extra space around them. To get a 2% margin, for example, invoke the macro with a parameter value of 2. (Min=0, Max=100%.)	0 (no margin)
TDEF Parameters		
SCALEX	The small panels can be scaled horizontally. To space them further apart, make them smaller with a value less than one (e.g. 0.9). (Min=0.0, Max=1.0.)	1 (no scaling)
SCALEY	The panels can also be scaled vertically. Horizontal and vertical scale factors can be different. (Min=0.0, Max=1.0.)	Same as SCALEX
XLATEX	The group of panels can be translated horizontally. (Min=0, Max=ABS(current value for Margin).) A negative number moves left; positive right.	0 (no translation)
XLATEY	The panels can also be vertically translated. Typically a value is assigned to XLateY to make more room for a title at the top of a page. If, for example, Margin is equal to 2, then setting XLateY to -1 effectively assigns a top margin of 3% to the graph. (Min=0, Max=ABS(current value for Margin).) A negative number moves down; positive up.	Same as XLATEX
COLOR	Color=border-color.	NONE
ROTATE	Rotate=degrees. The small panels are rotated. The title panel is not rotated.	0 (no rotation)
CLIP	Clip graphics at panel boundaries. (Valid values are "ON" and "OFF".)	OFF
Panel Coordinate Definition Parameters		
R1...RN	Number of panels in Row1 to RowN(rows). (Min=1, Max=8.)	NO Default
TREPLAY Call Parameter		
TREPLAY	A toggle for invoking the embedded TREPLAY macro. Valid values are "Y" and "N".	N (no)
Catalog ID Parameters		
IGOUT	Name of the input catalog: macro input.	WORK.GSEG
TC	Name of template catalog: macro output.	WORK.TEMPCAT
TNAME	Template name, i.e., template catalog entry: macro output.	TMPMAC

Table 3.3d *Parameters used by %TMPLT. Gray bands delimit types of parameters.*

In Table 3.3d parameters are listed along with their descriptions, ranges, and default values. Keyword parameters are used exclusively because with the defaults, arguments can sometimes be omitted in the macro calls. Ranges in Table 3.3d may also be somewhat arbitrary. Setting SCALEY to 0.0, for example, would effectively remove all the small panels from the display, but no minimum is officially set in the macro for this parameter.

MARGIN performs a singular function of putting a user-defined border around the collection of small plots in the graph. Typically, this is done to allow sufficient space for displaying the grand title. Parameters SCALEX through CLIP have the same names as their TDEF counterparts described in Chapter 2, "Working with GREPLAY." The Row Number parameters (Rn) are used for calculating panel coordinates, and IGOUT through TNAME allow the user to specify temporary or permanent catalogs. The default values are for a development-oriented WORK environment.

The following macro call (with results depicted schematically in Figure 3.3e) shows off the flexibility and clarity of %TMPLT:

```
%TMPLT(MARGIN=2,SCALEX=0.98, SCALEY=0.98, XLATEY=-1,
       R1=1, R2=2, COLOR=BLACK);
```

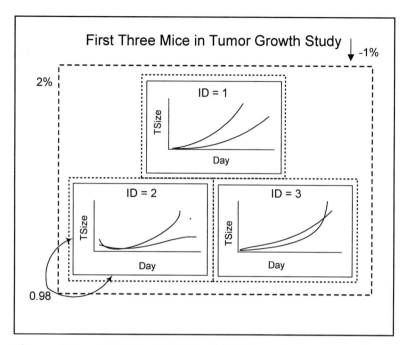

Figure 3.3e *MARGIN, SCALEY, SCALEX, and XLATEY work in concert to provide sufficient space for all graphic elements in a multiple-plot display.*

The values for the coordinate definition parameters, R1 and R2, are reversed in a subsequent call to %TMPLT to produce Figure 3.3f, having two plots in the first row and one in the second. In Figure 3.5b, later in the chapter, TREPLAY is used to left-justify a row of panels.

```
%TMPLT(MARGIN=3, SCALEX=0.95, SCALEY=0.95,
       XLATEY=-2.75, R1=2, R2=1);
```

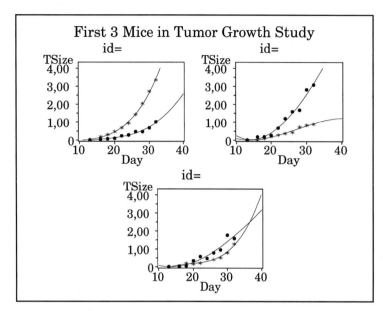

Figure 3.3f. *Two mouse plots are now in the first row, and one plot is centered by default in the second row.*

Values for the TDEF parameters, SCALEX, SCALEY, and XLATEY in the previous code, have been selected by trial and error. The TMPLT macro is very fast, so you can simply repeat program executions until you are satisfied with what you see. Note that the absolute value of –2.75 for XLATEY is less than 3, the value for MARGIN. Otherwise, the plots would be translated off the page!

More Information

For an example that shows how to create a permanent template catalog in %TMPLT, see Watts, 1998.

Code Description

A fully commented version of the source code can be found in the Appendix. The following listing concentrates mainly on how panel coordinates are calculated:

```
%macro TMPLT(Margin=0,ScaleX=1,ScaleY=1,   ❶
   XLateX=0,XLateY=0,
   R1=,R2=,R3=,R4=,R5=,R6=,R7=,R8=,
   color=NONE,rotate=0,clip=OFF,treplay=N,
   igout=work.gseg,tc=tempcat,tname=TmpMac);

%macro treplay;   ❷
   ...
```

```
    %mend treplay;

    %let margin2 = %sysevalf(2.0 * &margin);   ❸❹

/* Define coordinate definition macro variables*/   ❺
    %let MaxNCol= 0;
    %let NRows= 0;
    %let NPanels=0;
    %do i=1 %to 8;
      %if &&r&i ne %then %do;
        %let NROWS = &i;
        %if &&r&i gt &MaxNCol %then %let maxncol=&&r&i;
        %let NPanels = %eval(&NPanels + &&r&i);
      %end;
    %end;
    %let Npanels = %eval(&NPanels +1);

      proc greplay tc=&tc igout=&igout nofs;
        tdef &Tname
```

Code checking for parameter errors is not included here.

```
    %let height=%sysevalf((100-&Margin2.)/&NRows);   ❻
    %let width=%sysevalf((100-&Margin2.)/&MaxNCol);   ❻

    %let PanelNum=1;   %*-- PanelNum = panel number;
     %do row = 1 %to &NRows;
/*Calculate Y-Coordinates*/  ❼
         %do column = 1 %to &&R&row;
           %if &column = 1 %then %do;
             %if &row = 1 %then %do;
               %let y1=%sysevalf(100.0-(&margin ));
             %end;
             %else %do;
               %let y1 = &y2;   ❽
             %end;
             %let y2=%sysevalf(&y1-&height);
           %end;
/*Calculate X-Coordinates*/  ❾
           %if &column=1 %then %do;
             %let x1 = %sysevalf(50-(&&R&row/2*&width));
           %end;
           %else %do;
             %let x1 = &x2;   ❽
           %end;
           %let x2=%sysevalf(&x1+&width);
           &PanelNum / llx=&x1 ulx=&x1 urx=&x2 lrx=&x2   ❿
                       lly=&y2 uly=&y1 ury=&y1 lry=&y2
                       ScaleX=&ScaleX ScaleY=&ScaleY
                       XLateX=&XLateX XLateY=&XLateY
                       Rotate=&Rotate
           %if %upcase(&color) ne NONE %then Color=&Color;
           %if %upcase(&clip) ne OFF %then clip;

           %let PanelNum=%eval(&PanelNum+1);

       %end; %*-- column;
```

```
      %end; %*-- row;
         &PanelNum / llx=0 ulx=0 urx=100 lrx=100   ⓫
                     lly=0 uly=100 ury=100 lry=0;   ⓬
         Template &TName;   ⓭
      run;
   %mend TMPLT;

   %if %upcase(&treplay) eq Y %then %do;   ⓮
      %treplay;
   %end;
```

❶ %TMPLT is defined with keyword parameters. Note the use of default values.

❷ The macro %TREPLAY is discussed in Section 3.4.

❸ MARGIN2 = 2 X MARGIN is used for calculating the length and width of the individual panels.

❹ %SYSEVALF can handle floating point parameters.

❺ Coordinate definition macro variables are defined: MAXNCOL is the maximum number of plots in a row of plots. NROWS is the total number of rows in a graph, and NPANELS, needed in the TREPLAY macro, is the sum of R1 through R8 plus 1 for the grand title panel.

❻ HEIGHT and WIDTH are lengths of individual panels in percent.

❼ Calculate Y coordinates starting in the upper left-hand corner. This makes Y1 larger than Y2.

❽ Assign the current lower-Y coordinate to upper-Y coordinate of the panel in the next row. Similarly, assign the current right-X coordinate to the left-X coordinate of the panel in the next column.

❾ To center-justify the plots, calculate X coordinates for each row starting from the middle. Given MARGIN2 = 2*margin, and WIDTH = (100–margin2)/MaxNCol.

   E.g. 3 panels, no margin: width = (100–0)/3 = 33.3:

   ∴ X1 = 50–(3/2*33.3) yielding X1 = 0.

   E.g. 2 panels, 2% margin: width = (100–4)/2 = 48 :

   ∴ X1 = 50–(2/2*48) yielding X1= 2

❿ Write a column panel.

⑪ Write the grand title panel.

⑫ A semicolon (;) closes the TDEF statement.

⑬ Assign a template.

⑭ Execute the macro, %TREPLAY, depending on the value for the TMPLT macro parameter, &TREPLAY.

3.4 %TREPLAY Automates Treplay for %TMPLT

Purpose
Plots can be displayed through the newly created template with a TREPLAY statement. Because the option *n:n* described in Chapter 2 is not intuitive, however, mistakes such as the one displayed in Figure 3.4a are all too possible.

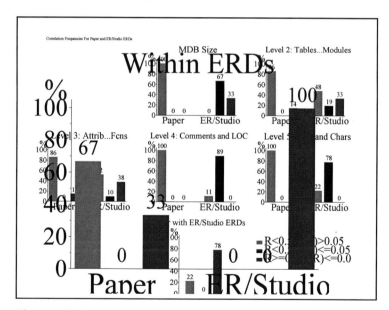

Figure 3.4a *First and last plots have been assigned to the wrong panels. Note the very small title in the upper left corner of the display.*

Furthermore, if multiple pages of graphs are to be generated, it is too easy to make mistakes with TREPLAY. For example, you have to enter the following code by hand to generate two pages of mouse tumor growth plots:

```
goptions display;
treplay  1:1    2:2    3:3    4:4
         5:5    6:6    7:7    8:8
         9:9   10:10  11:11  12:12
        13:13  14:14  15:15  16:16
        17:33;

treplay  1:17   2:18   3:19   4:20
         5:21   6:22   7:23   8:24
         9:25  10:26  11:27  12:28
        13:29  14:30  15:31  16:32
        17:33;
```

You have to remember that the last plot, plot #33, references the grand title, and it is replayed for each page of plots. Going from plot #16 to plot #33 on the first page is confusing.

Usage
Since %TREPLAY is contained completely within the TMPLT macro, just run it by assigning a value of 'Y' to the TREPLAY TMPLT macro parameter.

Code Description
Again, a fully commented version of the source code for the TMPLT macro can be found in the Appendix. Remember, the value for the macro variable, *npanels*, is calculated beforehand in the TMPLT macro.

```
%macro TREPLAY;
```

… Skip over method for determining the value for &nplots

```
proc greplay nofs igout=&igout tc=&tc;
Template &tname;
%let numgrafs=%sysfunc(ceil(&nplots./&npanels.) );   ❶
%let plot=1;   ❷
%do i= 1 %to &numgrafs;
   treplay
      %do panel=1 %to &npanels;   ❷
         %if &panel eq &npanels %then %do;   ❸
            &panel.:&nplots.
         %end;
         %else %if &plot lt &nplots %then %do;   ❹
            &panel.:&plot.
            %let plot=%eval(&plot + 1);
         %end;
      %end;
   ;   ❺
%end;
run;
%mend TREPLAY;
```

❶ The number of graphs is defined with the ceiling function to ensure that one plot beyond the maximum number of panels will go to a new page of graphs.

❷ Plots are summed over pages, whereas panels always start at 1 for a new page.

❸ Where the grand title panel is assigned the title plot.

❹ Where the remaining panels and plot assignments are accommodated.

❺ Prints the single semi-colon in the TREPLAY command.

3.5 Limitations of %TREPLAY

The TREPLAY macro does have some limitations that need to be mentioned. First, it cannot be used for writing multiple pages of output to a graphics stream file. More importantly, the macro generates plot assignments in a lock-step fashion. This means that panels are always center-justified. Therefore, if you want your plots to be right- or left-justified, you have to manually enter the TREPLAY statement into the your source code. Notice in the following code fragment, for example, that a plot is not assigned to the third panel in the template. This action moves the third plot one panel over to the right. (Remember **4:3** means that **plot #3** is assigned to **panel #4**.) It is also not possible to make the third plot a blank GSLIDE, since by-group processing is used to generate the mouse plots. GSLIDE either comes before or after all the mouse plots—not in-between. Look at Figure 3.5 to see how the code produces a second row of plots that is right-justified.

```
%TMPLT(Margin=3, XLATEY=-3,
        Scalex=0.95, Scaley=0.95
        NRows=2,MaxNCol=2,R1=2,R2=2);

treplay 1:1  2:2  4:3  5:4;
```

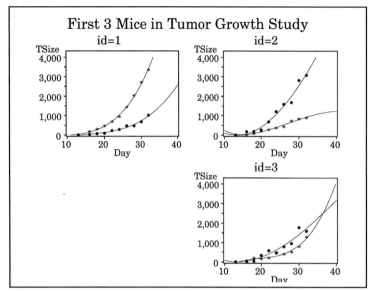

Figure 3.5   *%TREPLAY cannot be used to right-justify panels in a multiple-plot display.*

See Also

See Chapters 4 and 5 for the upper triangular scatterplot of baseball statistics that right-justifies a 5X5 square matrix of panels.

3.6 %SIZEIT Corrects Textual and Shape Distortion

Purpose

When plots are replayed through panels that do not conform to the default aspect ratio for your graphics device, both text and shapes can be distorted so significantly that the graph becomes unreadable. Figures 3.6a and 3.6b show distorted and undistorted versions of the Shannon measure of amino acid diversity for three different genes.

The Shannon score (H) ranges from 0 (no diversity) to near 4 (maximum diversity). There are 125 amino acids per gene replicate. The numbers in the plot titles show how many gene replicates are used for calculating each of the 125 values of H.

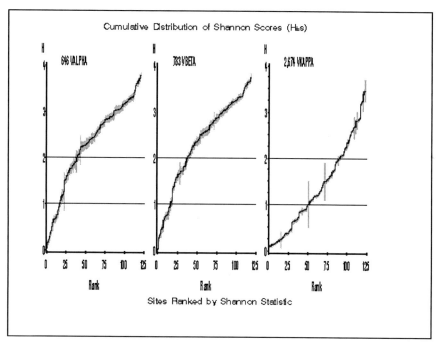

Figure 3.6a   *A screen snapshot of SAS/GRAPH output shows axes labels and plot titles that are almost unreadable.*

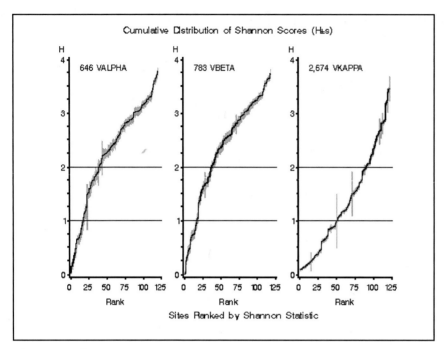

Figure 3.6b   *The distortion in Figure 3.5a is corrected with an application of the %SIZEIT macro.*

The circles in Figure 3.6c highlight shape distortion that was not evident in the Shannon graphs. The distortion is corrected in Figure 3.6d with an application of the SIZEIT macro.

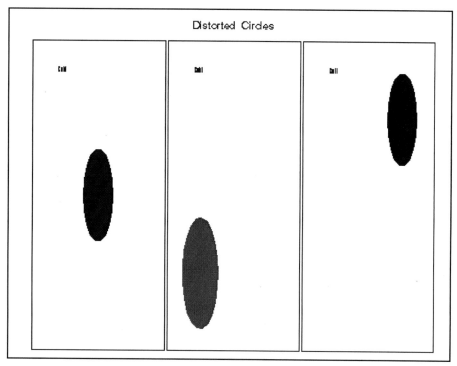

Figure 3.6c *Both shapes and text are distorted in this graph. The plot labels are illegible.*

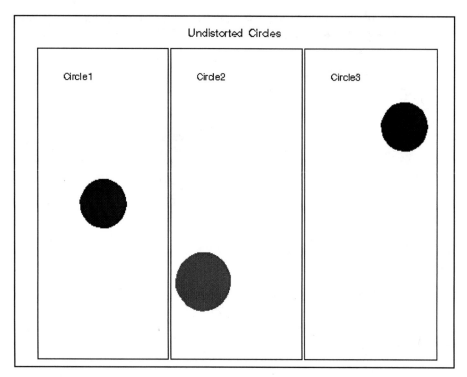

Figure 3.6d *Again, the SIZEIT macro is used to correct the shape and text distortion.*

Usage and Code Description

To correct image and text distortion, it is necessary to make the original plot the same size as the panel that replays it. All %TMPLT parameters and calculated macro variables related to size are re-used in %SIZEIT. They are listed along with two new parameters XMAX and YMAX in Table 3.6e below:

Parameter Definitions for %SIZEIT		
Parameter	**Description and Range**	**Default**
MARGIN	A border can surround the group of small, equal-sized panels on a page. If a value of 2 is entered, then a margin of 2% will surround the panels. (Min=0, Max=100%.)	0 (no margin)
SCALEX	The small panels can be scaled horizontally. To space them further apart, make them smaller with a value less than one (e.g., 0.9). (Min=0.0, Max=1.0.)	1 (no scaling)
SCALEY	The panels can also be scaled vertically. Horizontal and vertical scale factors can be different. (Min=0.0, Max=1.0.)	Same as SCALEX
NROWS	Number of rows containing panels. (Min=1, Max=8.) While calculated in %TMPLT, NROWS must be entered as a parameter in %SIZEIT.	NO Default Required entry
MAXNCOL	Maximum number of panels in a row of panels (no limit). Also calculated in %TMPLT, but entered as a parameter here.	NO Default Required entry
XMAX	Length of the horizontal axis for the graphics output area (device dependent).	NO Default
YMAX	Length of the vertical axis for the grahics output area (device dependent).	NO Default

Table 3.6e *Parameters to %SIZEIT are used to correct text and shape distortion in multiple-plot displays. Values for MARGIN, SCALEX, SCALEY, NROWS, and MAXNCOL should be identical to the values used in the TMPLT macro.*

Values for XMAX and YMAX are a function of the device that displays the graphic. For example, the GDEVICE procedure returns 10.667 and 8 inches for the WINPRTC driver and 11 and 8.5 inches for the CGMMW6C driver. The output from the macro is a GOPTIONS statement containing adjusted values for HSIZE and VSIZE for all the small, equal-sized panels in the display.

Figure 3.6f is a schematic that shows how %SIZEIT calculates HSIZE and VSIZE for the following macro call:

```
%SIZEIT(Margin=6, ScaleX=0.98, ScaleY=0.98,
   Nrows=1, MaxNCol=3, XMax=10.67, YMax=8.0);
```

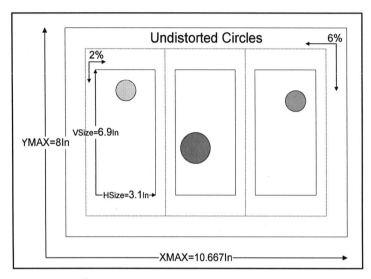

Figure 3.6f *A schematic that shows how VSIZE and HSIZE are calculated in %SIZEIT.*

The following statements perform the work of the macro:

```
%let margin2 = %sysevalf(2.0 * &margin);
%let Vsize = %sysevalf(((100-&Margin2)/&NRows)    ❶
                    * &ScaleY * &YMax *0.01);
%let Hsize = %sysevalf(((100-&Margin2)/&MaxNCol)
                    * &ScaleX * &XMax *0.01);
goptions vsize=&VSize in hsize=&Hsize in;    ❷
```

❶ Assign values to macro variables VSIZE and HSIZE.

❷ Output from the macro is a GOPTIONS statement containing values for VSIZE and HSIZE in inches.

Given the macro call above, the calculations for HSIZE and VSIZE are

```
HSIZE = (100-12)/3 X 0.98 X 10.67 X 0.01 = 3.1 inches
VSIZE = (100-12)/1 X 0.98 X 8.0   X 0.01 = 6.9 inches
```

Again, a commented version of the macro is included in the Appendix.

More Information

For a complete description of the causes for shape and text distortion, see Easter and Noto, 1995.

For a method to automatically correct distortion in a template definition macro, see Noto and Kalt, 1997. This is a nice enhancement.

3.7 Another Solution to the Distortion Problem

Another solution to the distortion problem shows that the %TMPLT macro has its limitations. In Figure 3.7 solid shapes and connecting lines are plotted with PROC G3D. The algorithm displayed in this graphic was used for superimposing the Shannon diversity scores discussed in Section 3.6 on a gene backbone having X, Y, and Z coordinates.

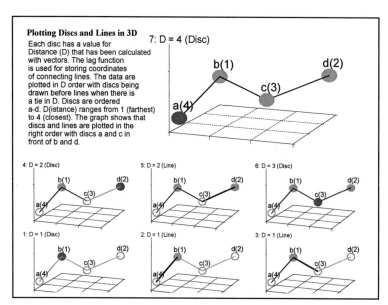

Figure 3.7 *Plotting solid discs with connecting lines requires a depiction of depth with points being plotted in the correct order from farthest to nearest. Hollow discs and light gray lines mean the object has not yet been drawn. Dark discs and thick lines point to the current object being added to the plot.*

While the discs are not circular in this graph, the discrepancy is hardly noticed because their shape is uniform in all the plots. Consistency is achieved because the plot in the upper right corner is exactly twice the size as the other plots in the graph. The small plots show a graph in progress. The large plot is the completed figure. An enlarged version of this graph can be found in the Appendix.

It would not be possible to generate this graph with the TMPLT macro, because the panels are different sizes. Panel coordinates have been entered by hand, leaving no room for a grand title at the top. At the same time, more control is gained over the placement of the plots on the page, with the Z-Axis being stretched in the small plots by increasing XLATEY to 1.2 in their assigned panels.

More Information

For a description of amino acid diversity that is illustrated in Figures 3.6a, 3.6b, and 3.7, see Watts and Litwin, 1992.

3.8 Putting It Together: Calling the Macros in the Right Order

To work properly, the macros must be called in the right order. Figure 3.8 shows where to position the macros in a calling program.

```
           Coordinating Macros and Program Statements
                      in a Calling Program

%DELGCAT(WORK.GSEG);
goptions device=win targetdevice=winprtc htext=2
   ftext=swiss nodisplay rotate=landscape;

%SIZEIT(margin=6, ScaleX=0.98, ScaleY=0.98, NRows=1,
   MaxNCol=3, YMax=8, XMax=10.667);

/*  Intervening  code  generates  small  plots  with
adjusted values for HSIZE and VSIZE */

goptions reset=goptions /*reset for grand title*/
goptions device=win targetdevice=winprtc htext=2
   ftext=swiss nodisplay rotate=landscape;

/* Create grand title with GSLIDE */

goptions display;
%TMPLT(margin=6, ScaleX=0.98, ScaleY=0.98, NRows=1,
   MaxNCol=3, R1=3, Color=black);
```

Figure 3.8 *Macro calls are displayed in their proper order in a calling program. Note that in Version 8, the graphics window **must** be closed after each program run. The call to %TREPLAY is not shown because it is issued as the last statement in %TMPLT. The graphics devices listed in the figure just happen to be for Windows. The macros work on any operating system.*

If the operating instructions above are carefully followed, the macros described in this chapter will conveniently generate a wide variety of multiple-plot displays. They accommodate a grand title with ease and offer a number of options for the placement of the individual plots on a page.

CHAPTER 4

Promoting Visual Thinning

4.1 What Is Visual Thinning, and How Is It Incorporated into Multiple-Plot Displays?

E.R. Tufte has suggested that the data-to-ink ratio is a measure of a graph's quality (Tufte 1983). In *SAS System for Statistical Graphics*, Michael Friendly extends Tufte's idea to the concept of *visual thinning* used in graphic design to

> allocate visual attention in a nonuniform way so as to focus attention on aspects of the data in relation to their worthiness for examination. The box plot is an example of this principle applied to the display of a single variable. For observations in the middle of the distribution, only the center and spread are portrayed collectively by the box; the whisker lines show the range of most of the data. Outside observations, which may need to be examined or set aside, are displayed individually, with more dramatic plotting symbols for points that are far outside (Friendly 1991, p. 39).

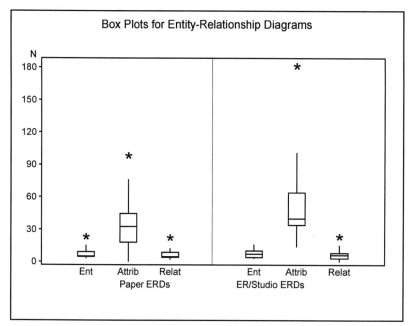

Figure 4.1   *SAS V8 enhanced box plots are used to compare counts of entities, attributes and relationships from manually generated (paper) Entity Relationship Diagrams (ERDs) with their Case Tool (ER/Studio) counterparts. ERDs from37 databases are compared.*

The outliers above the whiskers in the box plot are highlighted in Figure 4.1. For bolder plot symbols use value=*text-string*("*") font=*text-font* rather than value=*special-symbol* (star). The *T* option for drawing top and bottom horizontal lines on the whiskers has been omitted because no additional information is gained from adding these lines to the graph.

Friendly also applies visual thinning to a multiple-plot display by selectively omitting tick marks and axis labels from his baseball scatterplot matrix (Friendly, p.14). The same graph is thinned further in Section 4.4 with an application of the TMPLT macro, resulting in a more intuitively understood upper triangular matrix of plots. This alteration serves to reinforce the significance of Friendly's contribution: visual thinning promotes effective communication not only by eliminating distracting or redundant information from a graph but by selectively emphasizing key points that need to be made. The need to simplify the message increases when multiple plots are displayed on a single page.

While the TMPLT macro promotes visual thinning for the baseball graph, the emphasis here is on the techniques that can be used in the programs that call the GREPLAY extension macros. The macros reposition underlying panels whereas the techniques described in this chapter focus on the manipulation of viewable plot elements.

More Information

For the relationship between data-ink and graphical redesign, see Tufte 1983, pp. 90–105. Tufte defines the data-ink ratio as

$$\text{Data-ink ratio} = \frac{\text{data-ink}}{\text{total ink used to print the graphic}}$$

The higher the ratio, the better the graph according to Tufte, since the denominator in the equation also contains non-data items such as grid marks, axes lines, and labels. Tufte also adds unnecessary annotations defined as "chart junk" to the denominator of his equation. An example of chart junk would be the third dimension of a bar chart that fails to communicate any additional information to the viewer. It should be noted that Tufte simplifies by elimination; Friendly simplifies by elimination *and* emphasis. Additional examples cited in Section 4.2 should clarify the distinction.

See *SAS/GRAPH Software: Reference, Version 8*, pp. 226–43 for a description of the Symbol Statement, and pp. 273–75 for *Example 4. Creating and Modifying Box Plots*.

4.2 Mouse Plots Revisited

A review of the mouse plots shows that Tufte's data-to-ink ratio can be misapplied. Since eight mouse curves are displayed in a single plot in Figure 4.2a, the data-to-ink ratio is actually quite high. But the graph is unreadable. What needs to be applied to this graph is *data thinning*, not *visual thinning*.

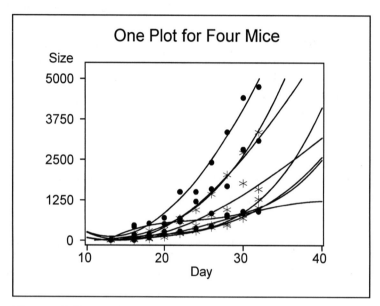

Figure 4.2a. *Left and right tumors for four mice are displayed together on a single graph. Since there is only one set of axes labels on the graph, the data-to-ink ratio is actually quite high. The ratio even receives an additional boost with the absence of identifying mouse labels. Unfortunately, the graph is not very informative.*

In Figure 4.2b, the data-to-ink ratio is lowered but the mouse plots are more visible. In Figure 4.2c, the inner axes and identification labels are either removed or simplified. As a result, not only does the data-to-ink ratio increase in Figure 4.2c, additional space becomes available for enlarged plots with thicker curves and bigger plot symbols. Here is an example of visual thinning where simplification and emphasis both play an important role in making the data the focus of the display.

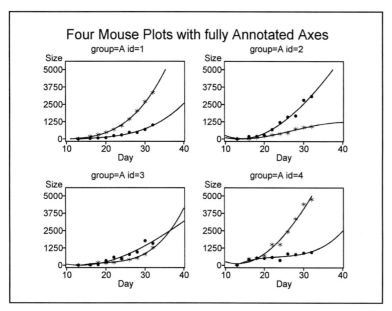

Figure 4.2b *While an application of %TMPLT improves the readability of the axes labels and leaves sufficient room for the title, the graph contains a lot of redundancy that could be eliminated with visual thinning.*

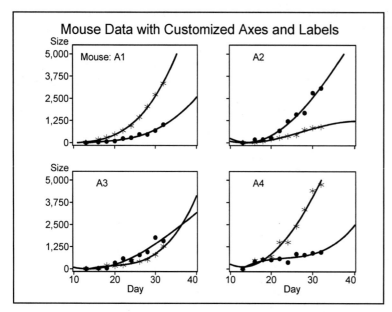

Figure 4.2c. *Visually thinned mouse plots with redundant text removed. Converting by-group labels to note statements enables the plots to be enlarged in this graph. Tumor size can also be formatted with a comma for increased readability.*

Unfortunately, the by-group processing used to create the fully annotated graph in Figure 4.2b will not work to eliminate redundancy from a multiple-plot display because different programming instructions must be issued for the marginal plots. The graph in Figure 4.2c is customized with a macro that uses a WHERE clause on PROC GPLOT to obtain the correct subset of the data. The following code is from the same macro that customizes and aligns the axes for the two 16-plot displays of all 32 mice in the study. The two full-sized graphs can be found in the Appendix.

```
%do plotnum=1 %to 32;
 %let mod16=%sysfunc(mod(&plotnum,16));   ❶
 %if &mod16 eq 0 %then %let mod16=16;
 %let mod4=%sysfunc(mod(&plotnum,4));   ❷

 *-- Y axis;
 %if &mod4 eq 1 %then %do;   ❷
     axis1 major=(h=.5cm w=30) w=30 minor=none
     order=(0 to 5000 by 1250) offset=(2,7)
     length=80pct   ❸
     label=("Size");
 %end;
 %else %do;
     axis1 major=(h=.5cm w=30) w=30 minor=none
     order=(0 to 5000 by 1250) offset=(2,7)
     length=80pct   ❸
     label=none value=none;
 %end;

 *-- X axis;
 %if &mod16 ge 13 %then %do;   ❶
     axis2 major=(h=.5cm w=30) w=30 minor=none
     order=(10 to 40 by 10)
     length=80pct origin=(20pct,17pct)   ❸ ❹
     label=("Day");
 %end;
 %else %do;
     axis2 major=(h=.5cm w=30) w=30 minor=none
     order=(10 to 40 by 10)
     length=80pct origin=(20pct,17pct)   ❸ ❹
     label=none value=none;
 %end;
%end;
```

❶ MOD16 identifies fourth row plots for X labels in two pages of plots. Also, when it equals 1, a conditional note statement in PROC GPLOT adds the word *Mouse* to the plot in panel #1 (source code not shown).

❷ MOD4 identifies first column plots for Y labels in two pages of plots.

❸ LENGTH fixes the length of the axes lines.

❹ ORIGIN sets the position of the origin. LENGTH and ORIGIN are needed for creating uniform plots insensitive to annotation with axes that are positioned at the same location in the graphics output area. ORIGIN only needs to be specified for one axis.

4.3 Format Optimization Study

Refuting a claim for efficiency with a set of multiple-plot displays proves to be a major challenge in the format optimization study. A judicious use of visual thinning along with supportive diagrams and text is needed to show that sequential formats ordered by start-value frequencies fail to keep up with their default binary counterparts when data from highly skewed distributions are formatted.

A sequential search is thought to enhance speed because initial start values in the format occur so frequently in the data. In contrast, the default binary format is assumed to be slower because the collating sequence of start values reflects nothing about the underlying structure of the data that are being formatted.

This method for improving efficiency is refuted in a set of graphs that show resolution times for binary, sequential, and two hybrid embedded formats superimposed on different skewed distributions of start values. The set of graphs is displayed in Figure 4.3.

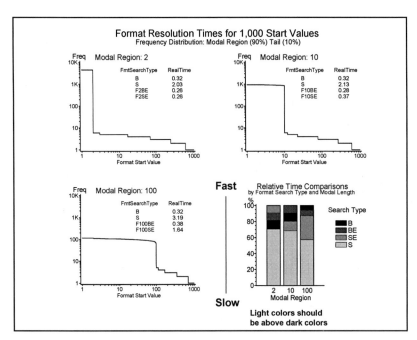

Figure 4.3. *The first three distribution plots use a step function to show that start values are discrete rather than continuous. Resolution times are listed as seconds in the distribution plots, and comparatively as percents in the bar chart. The fastest formats with the narrowest bands appear at the top of the bar chart.*

4.3.1 Visual thinning is implemented judiciously

Visual thinning in this example is accomplished by emphasis and not by removing graphic elements such as axes labels from the display. The log scale essential for displaying the distribution plots is a visual thinning tool because attention is focused in a nonuniform way on the smaller values of both axes. Without a log scale, one could not see that the high frequencies are restricted to two or ten out of 1,000 start values in the first two plots or that the curve of the distribution's tail rises above the horizontal axis line in all three plots. If the horizontal axis were linear, 10 out of 10,000 could not be distinguished from zero.

Emphasis on the smaller values, however, comes with a cost. The high concentration of observations in the modal regions of the distributions is minimized visually, and the length of the tails causing a slow-down for sequential searches is blunted.

A bar chart is also added to the display to emphasize the importance of the resolution times. Search types are ordered by speed with the fastest performers appearing at the tops of the bars. The placement of the formats within the bars shows again that the sequential format is slower than the others. Repetition, therefore, is also used in this example for emphasis.

Clarity remains elusive with this graph, because the metaphor "more is better" is contradicted by length of time as a measure of efficiency. Therefore the words "fast" and "slow" have been inserted next to the bar chart, and the statement "light colors should be above dark colors" reminds the viewer that the graph is refuting and not confirming assumptions tested in the study.

4.3.2 With visual thinning, graphs may not be self-explanatory

Axes and descriptive labels are abbreviated to keep extraneous text to a minimum in Figure 4.3. However, the abbreviations generate additional questions that must be answered. For example, nowhere is it explained that the initials **BE** and **SE** reference embedded format types or that distributions can be subdivided into *modal* and *tail* regions. The graph clearly is not self-explanatory. It needs to be enhanced by diagrams, tables, and descriptive text. Figure 4.3.2 is a diagram that graphically defines terms used in the format optimization study.

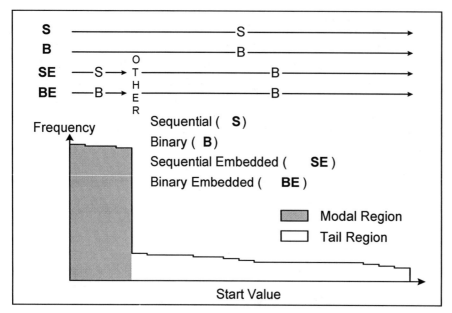

Figure 4.3.2. *The configuration of a skewed distribution is assumed to favor the sequential access method for labeling start values. The four formats are juxtaposed over the horizontal axis. Note that both embedded formats point to a binary search to process the long, sparsely populated tail region having a normal, not skewed distribution.*

Some time has been spent describing the Format Optimization Study to show that the construction of an informative graph is not always straightforward. You need to understand the principles of visual thinning and know when to use text and tables to supplement the message a graph is trying to convey. Trade-offs are also part of the package. Visual thinning leads to compact, easily understood presentations. Pruning shouldn't be so severe though that too many questions are left unanswered.

More Information

For a detailed example that orders subgroups by value in a stacked bar chart, see Redman, 1993. Her algorithm was used to create the bar chart in Figure 4.3a.

For a description of format concatenation that uses formats as labels, see Shoemaker, 1998. The labeled formats are also known as embedded formats.

For a complete description of the format optimization study, see Watts, *On the Relationship between Format Structure and Efficiency in SAS*, 2001. Timings for distributions with 100, 1,000, and 20,000 start values are tested.

4.4 Baseball Data

As an example of visual thinning, Michael Friendly presents a scatterplot matrix for baseball data represented as a nine-plot display in Figure 4.4a. To recapitulate from this chapter's introduction: tick marks and labels are not placed on the individual plots. Instead, all annotation is confined to the *key* or diagonal plots on the graph. There, axes labels are replaced by the row and column variable names, and the value labels are replaced by scale information (minimum and maximum values for each axis). The amount of text on the graph is significantly reduced by these techniques. Friendly also maximizes the size of the individual plots by directing the tick marks inwards. This clever maneuver simplifies the SAS code because there is no need to specify axes lengths or define an origin to maintain uniform plot sizes.

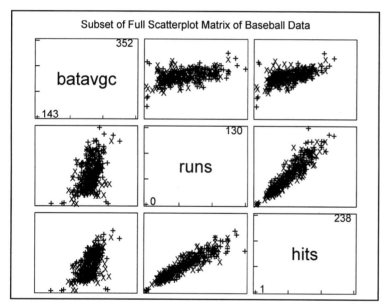

Figure 4.4a *Nine out of the original 25 plots in Friendly's scatterplot matrix are displayed. The paired transpositions are somewhat hard to identify because the plots are not replayed through square panels.*

The graph in Figure 4.4a is streamlined further by invoking TREPLAY outside of %TMPLT to right-justify a subset of the original plots. The right justification eliminates the redundant transpositions, leaving an upper triangular matrix with the same diagonal annotation as the original graph. The new graph is easier to read because the Y dimensions are obtained by consulting the diagonal plot to the left, and the X dimensions come from the lower diagonal plot. Figure 4.4b shows a portion of the upper triangular matrix. The full rendition can be found in the Appendix. Here is the SAS code needed for generating the matrix:

```
%TMPLT (Margin=2.5, XLateY=-2,   ❶
        ScaleY=0.95, ScaleX=0.95,
        TREPLAY=N,   ❷
        R1=5, R2=5, R3=5, R4=5, R5=5);
   goptions display;
treplay 1:1   2:2   3:3     4:4     5:5   ❸
              7:6   8:7     9:8    10:9
                   13:10   14:11   15:12
                           19:13   20:14
                                   25:15
              26:16;
quit;
```

❶   A call to %TMPLT builds a square matrix of 25 panels.

❷   The default value for the %TREPLAY parameter is specified to emphasize the fact that the TREPLAY macro is not invoked in this application.

❸   The TREPLAY statement is used to right-justify the plots. The command imitates the way the plots appear on the page. Only a slight alteration had to be made to Friendly's code to obtain the upper 15 plots from the original 25:

```
%do i = 1 %to &nvar;           /* rows */
  ...
  %do j = &i %to &nvar;     /* cols */  ❹
    ...
    %if &i = &j %then %do; /* diagonal plot */
      ...
    %end;
    %else %do              /* data plot*/
      ...
    %end;
  %end;
%end;
```

❹   The initial value of 1 (one) in the DO loop is replaced with the current value of the macro index variable, *i*.

The position of the minimum and maximum values is data-dependent in Figure 4.4b, whereas they were fixed at 6 and 95 percent of the *data output area* in Figure 4.4a. The change was made to visually illustrate why the points in the data plots do not span the full length of the axes. An examination of *Runs by Hits*, for example, shows that the data span the entire Y-axis but not the X-axis. The shortened range in the X-axis can be attributed to the discrepancy between the data maximum (238) and the axis range (0-300). Because the tick marks are not labeled, it is easy to become confused. Again, visual thinning must be exercised with care to make sure the graph conveys sufficient information to the viewer.

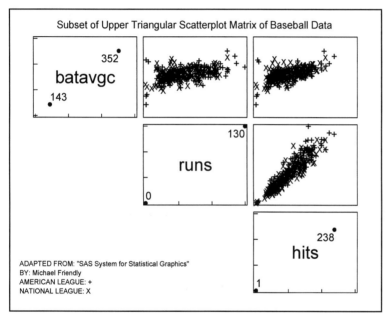

Figure 4.4b *The upper triangular matrix leaves plenty of room for additional annotation on the graph. The diagonals are uniform in appearance because they have four tick marks set with the major=(n=4) clause in the axes statements.*

The following fragment from the slightly altered Annotate DATA step *title* in Friendly's source code changes the values for XSYS and YSYS so that data points are displayed with one coordinate system and the variable names with another:

```
data title;
  length text style function $8;
  set minmax;
  style='XXXXXX'; function = 'LABEL';   ❶
  xsys = '1'; ysys = '1'; *variable names;   ❷
  x = 50; y = 50;   ❸
  text = "&vi";   ❹
  size = 1.5 * &nvar;   ❺
  output;

  style='XXXXXX'; function = 'LABEL';
  xsys='2'; ysys='2';      *data points;   ❷
  function='label';
  x = min; y = min; position = '3';   ❻
  text = left(put(min, best6.));
  size = 0.9 * &nvar;   ❺
  output;

  style='none'; function = 'symbol';
  text='dot'; color='black'; output;
  style='XXXXXX'; function = 'LABEL';
  x = max; y = max; position = '7';   ❻
  text = trim(put(max, best6.));
  size = 0.9 * &nvar;   ❺
  output;

  style='none'; function = 'symbol';
  text='dot'; color='black'; output;
  ...
run;
```

❶ The selection of style or font is arbitrary. Using hardware fonts sometimes reduces the size of the output graphics file.

❷ Coordinate systems are *abs % of data area* for the variable name (XSYS=YSYS=1) and *abs value of data area* for the data points and their labels (XSYS=YSYS=2).

❸ X=50; Y=50; places the variable name in the middle of the data area.

❹ Variable Name.

❺ More plots require a bigger size.

❻ Position is set to unspecified default center (5), left upper justify (3), and right lower justify (7).

More Information

For his scatterplot matrix, program, and input data, see Friendly 1991, pp. 13–14, 577–81, and 598–607.

For a complete review of the Annotate facility, see Carpenter 1999. In section 5.4.3, pp. 52–55, he creates an axis with different values for XSYS and YSYS variables.

4.5 Putting It Together: Applying a Macro for Visual Thinning in the Calling Program

The examples of visual thinning presented in this chapter show that it is accomplished by customizing the individual plots in a multiple-plot display. Only the first column and last row of plots in the mouse graph are assigned axes in Figure 4.2c, and the word "mouse" appears just once in the first plot on the page. Different plots are selectively annotated in Figure 4.3 for the Format Optimization study, and all axes labels are removed from an upper triangular matrix in the baseball graph in Figure 4.4b. Tick marks and scale information along the diagonals convey complete axes information about the baseball plots.

The key point here is that the plots are no longer treated uniformly. Slight differences have crept into the processing that must be managed by macros. The easy by-group processing attached to a single invocation of a graphics procedure no longer works. The Annotate facility cannot easily be combined with by-group processing, and it is no substitute for a macro. In fact, just the opposite is the case with macro variables often being used to construct Annotate data sets for customized displays.

Section 4.5.1 lists the steps the SMALLPLOT macro must accomplish to generate a set of customized small plots in a display. *Pre* and *Post* activities are also listed to put the macro into its proper context.

4.5.1 Tasks of the SMALLPLOT macro in a calling program

The SMALLPLOT macro produces visually thinned, customized graphs in the following steps. Steps with angle brackets (<>) are optional. Creating an Annotate data set, for example, can be omitted when the graph is only labeled with constant text.

Pre-Macro

Header comments describe macro parameters that identify data sets and constant text displayed in a fixed location with a note statement.

LIBNAME statements if not set with macro parameter values.

SMALLPLOT Macro

The SMALLPLOT macro creates small plots either one at a time by separate macro invocations or all at once by a looping structure.

```
%macro SMALLPLOT(parm1, parm2, ... parmn);
```

<1>	If necessary, define global macro variables and complete LIBNAME statements with macro parameters.
2	Identify and manipulate the data for %SMALLPLOT to display.
<3>	Obtain values for data-derived macro variables that are displayed on the plot. These values cannot be communicated to the macro by parameter.
4	Define graphics elements (symbols, line widths, tick sizes etc.)
5	Build customized axes or rebuild UNIFORM axes.
<6>	Create an Annotate data set for graphics elements that are inserted into a plot at run-time.
7	Run the SAS/GRAPH procedure. Optionally, annotate it with note statements displaying parameter values.

```
%mend SMALLPLOT;
```

Post-Macro sequence of macro calls

```
goptions reset=goptions;
goptions ... nodisplay;
%DELCATMAC(...);
%SIZEITMAC(...);
%SMALLPLOT(...);
```
Create grand title plot (PROC GSLIDE)

```
%TMPLATMAC(...);
goptions ... display;
%TREPLAYMAC(...)
```

4.5.2 How Annotate data sets are used in this book

Annotate data sets are used to streamline graphics displays. They are not found in the mouse tumor growth programs. Instead, NOTE statements in PROC GPLOT are used to identify the mice, and conditional axes statements described in Section 4.2 customize the display.

Since annotations in graphs are sometimes hard to identify, this section points out the features from the graphs that have been annotated along with the relevant material by page number in Art Carpenter's *Annotate: Simply the Basics:*

Kaplan-Meier Curves: Figures 1.2a–1.2c

Strata are identified with one-character labels at the end of the curves. Log-rank and Wilcoxon chi-square statistics are also displayed using Annotate, but they could have been displayed using a note statement attached to PROC GPLOT.

Carpenter references: pp. 15–17, 23–25, 30–31, and 42–45.

Shannon Scores: Figures 3.6a–3.6b

The light gray standard deviations are actually bars drawn with Annotate macros. See the enlarged graph in the Appendix.

Carpenter references: pp. 72–80.

Plotting Discs and Lines in 3-D: Figure 3.7

Except for the grid and axes lines, PROC G3D has been replaced in its entirety by output from an Annotate data set. Shapes plotted include the DOT and CIRCLE *symbols,* and LINES. Functions employed are LABEL, SYMBOL, MOVE, and DRAW. Also included is the WHEN='AFTER' function that tells SAS/GRAPH to annotate after the plot has been generated.

Carpenter references: All for the Kaplan-Meier curves plus pp. 26–28 and 50–51.

Bar Charts in the Format Optimization Graphs: Figure 4.3

The legend is re-created with an Annotate data set so that the stacked bar chart can be ordered by value rather than by collating sequence.

Carpenter references: The same for the Shannon scores describing the Annotate macros.

Upper Triangular Matrix of Baseball Scores: Figures 4.4a and 4.4b

Output from an Annotate data set is used for labeling the diagonal plots with variable names and scale information.

Carpenter references: pp. 15–17, 23–25, 42–48, and 52–55.

It should be obvious by now that many iterations and an attention to detail are required to produce an informative graph. The GREPLAY extension macros take the drudgery out of the iterative process, and visual thinning provides a means for effective communication. Tufte (1983) equates the creation of a good graph to writing:

> Just as a good editor of prose ruthlessly prunes out unnecessary words, so a designer of statistical graphics should prune out ink that fails to present fresh data-information. Although nothing can replace a good graphical idea applied to an interesting set of numbers, editing and revision are as essential to sound graphical design work as they are to writing. (p. 100)

See Also

See Section 5.1 for a code review of the Kaplan-Meier curves that identifies the tasks from Section 4.5.1 by number.

CHAPTER 5

Incorporating ODS into Multiple-Plot Displays

5.1 The Survival Plots Revisited

The program KM2STRATA.SAS with macro *KM2* is selectively reviewed in this section to show how the Output Delivery System (ODS) is used to generate survival plots annotated with log-rank and Wilcoxon chi-square test results. More specifically, the following tasks are covered, which are adapted from the tasks of the SMALLPLOT macro as discussed in Section 4.5.1:

Pre-Macro tasks

% KM2 parameters are described and identified where they appear on a plot

Macro tasks

<1>	No global macro definitions or library assignments are used in the macro.
2	Use ODS to create input data sets. Create plot data in a DATA step.
3	Obtain log-rank and Wilcoxon chi-square statistics for display.
4	Generate a variable number of SYMBOL statements for plotting purposes. The SYMBOL statements reflect the presence or absence of censored observations in a data set.
5	Re-build UNIFORM axes by obtaining the maximum time on study and by calculating an increment variable for the ORDER option in the AXIS statement.
6	Show how the Annotate facility is used to label the strata.
7	Show how the GPLOT procedure customizes a graphic with additional annotations.

The post-macro sequence of macro calls discussed in Section 4.5.1 are not covered here, but steps 2–7 from the SMALLPLOT macro are reviewed to help you fully understand the role the calling program plays in generating customized graphics. The complete program listing for KM2STRATA.SAS can be found in SAS Online Samples.

5.1.1 KM2 parameters

The KM2 macro parameters are described in Table 5.1.1 and displayed in Figure 5.1.1.

Parameter	Description	Default
LIBNAME	Identifies the LIBNAME associated with the SAS data set (SDS).	None
SDS	Input SAS data set with variables: &STIME &&CENSOR &STRATVBL &GRPVBL	None
STIME	Variable name for survival times	SURVTIME
CENSOR	For status: dead or alive (censored)	DORA
STRATVBL	Data set name for Stratum variable	None
GRPVBL	Data set name for Group variable	None
GRPVAL	GRPVBL value that identifies the plot	ALL
XLBL	Labels the time units on the X-axis	"Time (months)"
YLBL	Labels the SURVIVAL Function in the Y-axis (usually "Survival")	SURVIVAL
ABBSTRT1	Abbreviation for labeling stratum #1	None
ABBSTRT2	Abbreviation for labeling stratum #2	None
FIRSTTIME	When true (1), the X-axis coordinates are calculated for all the plots on a graph.	0

Table 5.1.1 *Parameters associated with the KM2 macro in KM2STRATA.SAS. A default value of "none" means that the value is supplied at run-time.*

Figure 5.1.1 shows how parameter values for the following calls to the KM2 macro are translated into viewable plot elements:

```
%KM2 (libname=BBUData, sds=VALung,
      StratVbl=therapy, GrpVbl=Cell, GrpVal=Large,
      xlbl=Time(Days), ylbl=Survival,
      AbbStrt1=S, AbbStrt2=T,
      FirstTime=1);
```

and

```
%KM2 (libname=BBUData, sds=VALung,
      StratVbl=therapy, GrpVbl=Cell, GrpVal=Squamous,
      xlbl=Time(Days), ylbl=Survival,
      AbbStrt1=S, AbbStrt2=T);
```

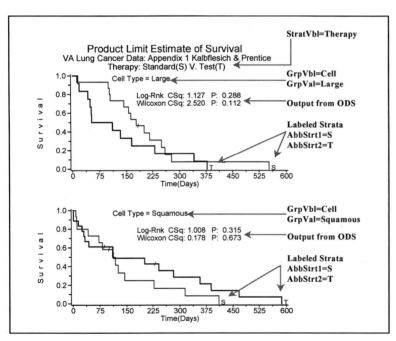

Figure 5.1.1 *Kaplan-Meier plots annotated with KM2 macro parameters.*

5.1.2 Macro task: processing the input data set with ODS

Historically, product limit estimates could be could be saved to the data set associated with the OUTSURV option in a PROC LIFETEST statement. However, there was no way to capture log-rank and Wilcoxon chi-square results except through an application of the PRINTTO procedure. With Version 8, both data sets can be generated in one call to ODS:

```
ods listing close;
ods output clear;
ods output ProductLimitEstimates = PLE&GrpVal  ❶  ❷
          (keep=stratum &StratVbl &Stime  ❸
              censor survival &GrpVbl);
ods output HomTests = HT&GrpVal  ❶  ❷
          (keep=test ChiSq ProbChiSq);  ❸

  proc lifetest data=subset method=km;  ❹
    time &Stime.*&Censor.(0);
    id &GrpVbl;
    strata &StratVbl;
  run;

ods listing;
ods output close;
```

❶ There are a number of options available for determining the names of ODS tables (object classes):

   a Consult the *SAS/STAT User's Guide*. Each procedure contains a list of ODS Table names. For PROC LIFETEST, the list of 21 tables can be found in Volume 2, pages 1830–31.

   b If confused by the list, exercise the following code in a separate program to associate table names with procedure output in the Output window:

```
ods listing;
ods trace on / listing;
  title 'VA Lung Cancer Data';
  proc lifetest data=bbu.VALung;
    time &Stime.*&Censor.(0);
    id cell;
    strata therapy;
  run;
ods trace off;
```

For a listing that identifies the table name associated with homogeneity tests, see Figure 5.1.2a.

   c The Results Window in SAS Explorer provides only the Table LABEL, not its NAME, because an object or data set has not yet be created; i.e., an output destination has not been specified in **b** above.

❷ Instances or objects of ODS tables ProductLimitEstimates and HomTests are declared. They are data sets PLE&GRPVAL and HT&GRPVAL. Since &GRPVAL identifies the plot that is being created, its text is appended to the data set names. (See Table 5.1.1 and Figure 5.1.1.)

❸ KEEP data set options can be issued even though the data sets are not created until after PROC LIFETEST runs. To learn what to keep, create prototype data sets PLE and HT by running PROC LIFETEST without the KEEP statement but with an output destination. Then follow either of these steps:

a Double-click on the object in the Results Window of SAS Explorer, and go to the column of interest in the ViewTable window. Right-click on it and select **Column Attributes** to find the variable name in the **Name** field. See the screen snapshot for the prototype data set HT in Figure 5.1.2b.

b If the clicking becomes onerous, the following SQL statement provides the necessary information:

```
proc sql;
    select memname, name, type
    from dictionary.columns
    where libname eq 'WORK' and
          memname in ('PLE', 'HT')
    order by memname, name;
```

Again, PLE and HT are the prototype data sets created beforehand.

ODS automatically creates variables with the same names as the arguments for the ID and STRATA statements in PROC LIFETEST. Therefore, variables &GRPVBL (cell) and &STRATVBL (therapy) can be found in the data set.

❹ The data set *subset* is created earlier in the program with

```
data subset;
  set &libname..&sds
  (where=(upcase(&GrpVbl.) = upcase("&GrpVal.")));
run;
```

LIBNAME and SDS are macro parameters. UPCASE on the left side of the equation converts the data set values to upper case whereas UPCASE on the right side converts the parameter value to upper case. Both are needed for a proper match.

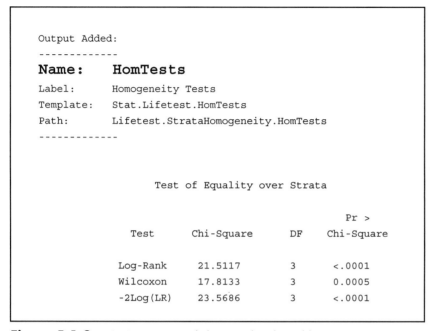

Figure 5.1.2a *ODS trace record showing that the Table Name **HomTests** is associated with Homogeneity Tests.*

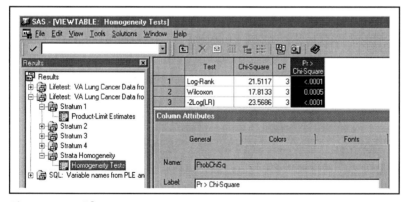

Figure 5.1.2b *Screen snapshot that shows the variable name in the HomTests table **HT** for Pr>Chi-Square is **ProbChiSq**. Note that the names in the Results Window correspond to ODS labels and not to the actual table names or objects.*

Curves from the ODS ProductLimitEstimates data set, PLE&GRPVAL, additionally need to be defined for plotting purposes. Therefore, a new data set, PLOT, replaces PLE&GRPVAL:

```
data plot(keep = &StratVbl stratum curve &STime      ❶
                 censor survival);
  retain retsurv;   ❷
  set PLE&GrpVal;
  by STRATUM notsorted;
  if survival ne . then retsurv=survival;   ❷
  curve=stratum;
  if CENSOR eq 1 then survival=retsurv;   ❷
  if last.STRATUM and CENSOR eq 1 then do;   ❸
    CENSOR=0;
    output;
    CENSOR=1;
  end;
  if CENSOR eq 1 then curve=curve+0.1;   ❹
  if survival ne . then output;   ❷
run;
```

❶ &STRATVBL is used by the Annotate facility later in the program. A STRATUM statement contains up to two CURVEs: one for events (CENSOR=0), the other for censors (CENSOR=1). &STIME appears on the X-axis whereas SURVIVAL ranges from 0.0 to 1.0 on the Y-axis.

❷ RETSURV for *retain-survival* is needed because values for SURVIVAL are set to MISSING for censored observations. RETSURV is reset every time SURVIVAL holds a non-missing value. When missing values for SURVIVAL occur for censored observations, they are replaced with the most recently assigned value for RETSURV. Because the first value in a stratum for SURVIVAL is always 1.0, there is no danger that the value of SURVIVAL for a censored observation will be incorrectly assigned. The last IF before the RUN statement accommodates missing values arising from tied SURVIVAL values for non-censored observations (EVENTS) occurring at the same time. There is no need to write the duplicates out to the PLOT data set.

If the original data set had been produced by the OUTSURV option for PROC LIFETEST, values for SURVIVAL would never be missing. ODS, therefore, does not fully imitate its predecessors.

❸ The curve for events (CENSOR=0) is drawn with a step function whereas censors are noted with a forward slash on top of the curve. When the last event is a censor, a connecting line has to be drawn to the final slash mark.

❹ As mentioned earlier, the collection of disconnected censor marks is also defined as a curve in SAS/GRAPH. Therefore, up to four curves can be created for the two strata:

STRATUM	CENSOR	CURVE	Maps To
1	0	1.0	symbol1
1	1	1.1	symbol2
2	0	2.0	symbol3
2	1	2.2	symbol4

Strata always contain events; censors may or may not be present. In the above scenario, four symbol statements aligned to the curves are created for the PROC GPLOT statement:

```
plot survival*&STime=curve;
```

More Information

See Chapter 15, "Using the Output Delivery System," pp. 255–300, in *SAS/STAT User's Guide, Version 8*. The examples are particularly helpful.

See Yourdon et. al., 1995, Chapter 2, "Fundamental Object-Oriented Concepts and Principals," pp. 12–19.

5.1.3 Macro task: obtaining log-rank and Wilcoxon chi-square statistics for display

After the homogeneity tests data set is created, macro variables containing test results are generated with the SYMPUT routine for later display through the Annotate facility:

```
data  null ;
  set HT&GrpVal.;
  if test eq 'Log-Rank' then
    call symput('LOGRnk','Log-Rnk CSq: '||        ❶
                left(put(chisq,8.4))||
                'P: '|| put(ProbChiSq,6.4));

  else if test eq 'Wilcoxon' then
    call symput('WILCOX','Wilcoxon  CSq: '||       ❶
                left(put(chisq,8.4))||
                'P: '|| put(ProbChiSq,6.4));
run;
```

❶ The LOGRNK assignment of `"Log-Rnk Csq: 1.127 P: 0.288"` appears as a label in Figure 5.1.1 by way of the Annotate facility:

```
size=2.75; xsys='1'; ysys='1';
x=30; y=78; text="&LOGRNK"; output;
x=30; y=72; text="&WILCOX"; output;
```

See Also

See Carpenter references to *Annotate: Simply the Basics* listed in Section 4.5.2.

See Section 5.1.6 for a description of how the Annotate facility is used to label the strata.

More Information

See Carpenter, 1998, Section 6.1, "Using the SYMPUT Routine," pp. 67–69.

5.1.4 Macro task: generating a data dependent number of SYMBOL statements for plotting curves

---

As mentioned previously, there can be anywhere from two to four curves on a plot. Each curve is assigned a symbol.

Code for creating symbol definitions:

```
proc sort data=plot out=splot nodupkey;  ❶
  by curve CENSOR;
run;
%let ticksize=3;
data _null_;
  retain multiple 5;
  set splot end=last;
  by curve CENSOR;
  iter+1;
  if CENSOR =0 then do;
    solidw=iter*multiple;  ❷
    call symput('sstr'||left(put(iter,2.)),  ❸
      "c=black i=steplj v=none l=1 w="
      ||left(put(solidw,2.))||";");
  end;
  else do;
    call symput('sstr'||left(put(iter,2.)),  ❹
    "c=black i=none font=swiss v=/ h=&ticksize;");
  end;
  if last then
    call symput('maxit',right(put(iter,2.)));
run;
```

❶ NODUPKEY results in a data set containing anywhere from two to four records—one per symbol.

❷ How variable width lines are assigned to the strata.

❸ In this example &SSTR1 is set to `c=black i=steplj v=none l=1 w=5;`

❹ In this example &SSTR2 is set to `c=black i=none font=swiss v=/ h=3;`

Double quotation marks are required in the SYMPUT statement for SSTR2 because the symbol string contains a second macro variable TICKSIZE that resolves to 3 in this particular instance.

Code for assigning symbol definitions:

```
%do j=1 %to &maxit;
  symbol&j;  ❶
  symbol&j &&sstr&j  ❷
%end;
```

❶ Each symbol definition is canceled prior to redefinition so that additional plots containing a different number and pattern of symbols can be plotted on the same graph.

❷ &&STR&j contains the new symbol definitions SSTR1 and SSTR2.

5.1.5 Macro task: rebuild UNIFORM axes that mimic by-group processing

The first time the macro KM2 is called, a uniform X-axis for all plots has to be constructed. The following code calculates values for MAXTIME, INCR, and FUZZ. MAXTIME and INCR are used in the ORDER option of the AXIS statement, and FUZZ supplies an offset for the strata labels.

```
%if &firsttime eq 1 %then %do;
  data _null_ ;
    array limit(11)  _temporary_
    (10,20,50,100,200,500,600,1000,2500,5000,10000);
    array _incr(11) _temporary_    ❶
    (1, 2, 5, 10, 25, 50, 75, 100, 250, 500, 1000);
    retain maxtime Nincr 0;
    set local.&psd. end=eof;    ❷
    if &STime gt maxtime then maxtime=&STime;
    if eof=1 then do;
      do i=1 to dim(limit);
        if maxtime lt limit[i] then do;    ❸
          incr = _incr[i];    ❶
          Nincr = ceil(maxtime/incr);
          maxtime = Nincr*incr;
          leave;
        end;
      end;
      if Nincr eq 0 then
        put "MAXTIME Error";
      else do;
        fuzz=0.01*maxtime
        call symput('maxtime',put(maxtime,5.));
        call symput('incr',put(incr,4.));
        call symput('fuzz',put(fuzz,best8.));
      end;
    end;
  run;
%end;
```

❶ To improve program readability, use a leading underscore for arrays when it makes sense to assign a scalar the same name as the aggregate data type.

❷ The value for MAXTIME is not based on the first subset but on the entire input data set.

❸ A LESS THAN condition takes care of the situation when the maximum value of the data coincides with an incremental value. With FUZZ, strict equality would result in the truncation of a stratum label.

With the vertical axis always ranging from 0.0 to 1.0, the UNIFORM by-group option is replicated in the macro with the addition of the following ORDER= option for the horizontal axis statement alone:

```
order=(0 to &maxtime by &incr)
```

More Information
See Leighton, 1994, for the definitive work on arrays.

5.1.6 Macro task: how the Annotate facility labels the strata

Recall that the strata labels are placed relative to the X and Y coordinates of the last points in each stratum.

```
data anno(keep=style function size xsys ysys
              position text x y);
  length function style $8 text $40;
  retain style 'swiss' function 'label' position '6';   ❶
  set plot end=last;
  by &StratVbl notsorted;
  if last.&StratVbl then do;
    size=2; xsys='2'; ysys='2';   ❷
    if STRATUM EQ 1 THEN text="&AbbStrt1";   ❸
    else text="&AbbStrt2";   ❸
    x=&STime + &fuzz.;   ❹
    if CENSOR eq 0 then y=0.015;   ❺
    else y=survival;   ❻
    output;
  end;
```

❶ Left-justify the label.

❷ Absolute data value coordinate system.

❸ Strata labels are macro parameters.

❹ X coordinate has an offset as discussed earlier.

❺ Last observation is an EVENT: looks like **| T**

❻ Last observation is a CENSOR: looks like ——**/ T**

5.1.7 Macro task: additional annotations in the GPLOT procedure

The calling program's final task is to create a plot with the GPLOT procedure. PROC GPLOT uses the PLOT data set derived from the ODS ProductLimitEstimates table and displays labels supplied to Annotate from the HomTests table. By using a NOTE rather than a TITLE statement for additional annotation, the plot gains a larger area for display on the Y-axis.

```
proc gplot annotate=anno data=plot;
   plot survival*&STime=curve / vaxis=axis1
                                haxis=axis2
                                nolegend
                                noframe;   ❶
   format survival 3.1;
   format &STime 4.;
   title1;
   note h=5 move=(20,95) angle=0  ❷
      "&GrpVbl = &GrpVal";
run;
```

❶ For Version 8, the default is a frame.

❷ A NOTE statement mimics the BY line and identifies the plot by the GROUP variable. In Figure 5.1.1 the values of the assigned notes are *Cell Type = Large* and *Cell Type = Squamous*.

5.2 Using ODS to Drill Down to Enlarged Plots

Despite efforts to streamline a multiple-plot display with visual thinning, there are times when a single plot or a subset of plots needs to be examined in greater detail. The TMPLT macro and Web output through ODS are used for generating drill-down graphs that are mapped to targeted enlargements.

5.2.1 Enlarging the baseball plots

Individual points in the baseball data can be examined in greater detail when a single scatter plot is enlarged and displayed with its corresponding diagonal plots. Figures 5.2.1a and 5.2.1b show how to drill down to an enlargement for Runs By Salary.

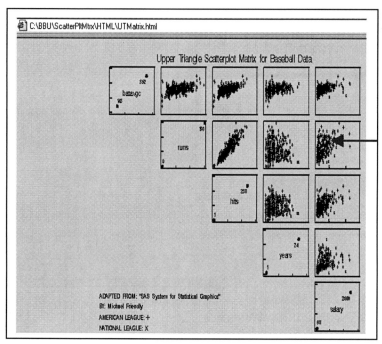

Figure 5.2.1a *The screen snapshot shows scatter plots with image maps that link the small plots to their enlargements. Diagonal plots do not have links.*

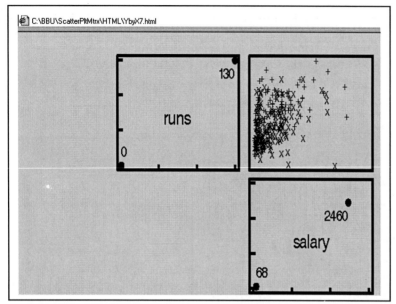

Figure 5.2.1b *Clicking on a point near the arrow in Figure 5.2.1a brings up this enlargement. The diagonal plots are not contiguous in the original display.*

To create a drill-down graph, a filename that references what SAS calls a *'path-to-Web-server'* or subdirectory must first be defined. The subdirectory is the repository for all HTML and GIF files generated by the program. The GOPTIONS statement references the subdirectory in the GSFNAME graphics option and sets the device to HTML. The initializing code appears as follows:

```
filename webout 'c:\BBU\ScatterPltMtrx\HTML';   ❶
goptions reset=global gunit=pct
ftext=swiss rotate=landscape;

goptions gsfname=webout device=html;   ❶
```

❶ Even though the LIBNAME statement often references a subdirectory and the FILENAME statement is reserved for a single file, their roles are somewhat blurred in a web application.

Links are added to the code in the calling program's macro. Links contain HREFs (Hypertext references) that point to targeted locations—in this example they point to other HTML files found in WEBOUT, the *path-to-web-server*. In the baseball program, links are only added to the data sets that support non-diagonal plots. The diagonal plots are by-passed with an IF statement:

```
%let linknum=1;
%do i=1 %to &nvar;
   ...
   %do j=&i %to &nvar;
      ...
      %if &i=&j %then %do;   ❶
      ...
      %end;
      %else %do;
        data subset(keep= &vi &vj &group links);   ❷
          length links $40;      ❸
          set &data;
          links="href="||quote("YbyX&linknum..html");   ❸
        run;

        symbol1 c=black i=none font=swiss v=+ h=8;
        symbol2 c=black i=none font=swiss v=X h=7;

        proc gplot data = subset imagemap=dummymap;   ❷ ❹
          plot &vi * &vj = &group / frame
                                    nolegend
                                    vaxis=axis1
                                    haxis=axis1
                                    html=links;   ❺

        axis1 label=none value=none major=none
              minor=none w=10 offset=(2);
        run;
        %let linknum = %eval(&linknum + 1);
      %end;
   %end;
%end;
```

❶ Annotated diagonal plots are created here. No links are added to them.

❷ The data set SUBSET is new to this application. Every data point in a single scatter plot is a hotspot that contains a link to the same destination HTML file. The hotspots are persistent. However, in the enlarged HTML target file they serve no purpose because the source and destination HREFs are the same.

❸ If the macro variable LINKNUM were not present, all possible link values would have to be processed by a SELECT statement. An example of an assignment in such a situation would be

```
when('2') links='href="YbyX2.html"';
```

❹ SAS writes coordinates of each of the data points to an image map defined within <MAP> tags in the HTML file. The assigned value DUMMYMAP does not appear elsewhere in the SAS source code or in the HTML code. To view the HTML source code, go into a Web browser such as Internet Explorer, bring up the HTML file, select the View menu, and then select Source. Here is a sample of the HTML code with map tags containing the coordinates SAS has calculated:

```
<MAP NAME="idx_map">
    <AREA SHAPE="RECT" href="YbyX10.html"
COORDS="375,302,378,308 " >   <AREA SHAPE="RECT"
                              href="YbyX10.html"
COORDS="362,310,365,317 " >   <AREA SHAPE="RECT"
                              href="YbyX10.html"
...many points later
COORDS="137,47,143,54 " >   <AREA SHAPE="RECT"
                            href="YbyX1.html"
COORDS="118,58,123,66 " ></MAP>
```

❺ Where the actual linking occurs.

After the plots with links have been created, additional interactions among GOPTIONS statements, the TMPLT macro, and ODS are required for building a hierarchy of linked graphs:

```
goptions reset=goptions;
goptions transparency noborder  ❶
    xmax=5.75in ymax=4in  ❷
    gsfname=webout device=GIF;  ❸ ❹

%Tmplt(Margin=2.5, XLateY=-2.5,  ❺
       ScaleY=0.95, ScaleX=0.95,
       R1=5, R2=5, R3=5, R4=5, R5=5);
    ods html body='UTMatrix.html' path=webout;  ❻
        treplay 1:1   2:2   3:3    4:4     5:5
                      7:6   8:7    9:8    10:9
                           13:10  14:11  15:12
                                  19:13  20:14
                                         25:15
              26: 16;

quit;  ❼
ods html close;  ❻

%Tmplt(Margin=2, R1=2, R2=2);  ❺

%macro zoom(num,treplay);  ❽
    ods html body="YbyX&num..html" path=webout;
    treplay &treplay;
    ods html close;
%mend zoom;

%zoom(1,%str(1:1 2:2 4:6));  ❽
%zoom(2,%str(1:1 2:3 4:10));
...
%zoom(10,%str(1:13 2:14 4:15));

ods listing;
quit;  ❼
```

❶ When the transparency option is set, the graph has the same background color as the browser.

❷ XMAX and YMAX are set to avoid the need for scrolling inside the browser to see the entire graph.

❸ WEBOUT is the destination directory for GIF and HTML output.

❹ The device has switched from HTML for generating links to GIF for creating images.

❺ Successive calls to %TMPLT with fewer defined panels enable the developer to create zoomed graphs with ease.

❻ With the ODS BODY option HTML files can be named. Otherwise, with DEV=HTML only index.html is produced and subsequently overwritten.

❼ The QUIT statement references PROC GREPLAY invoked inside the TMPLT macro. It is important not to issue QUIT statements from the ZOOM macro. Otherwise, subsequent calls to TREPLAY will not work. QUIT and ODS operate independently from each other.

❽ The TREPLAY parameter for ZOOM always contains three plot references: one for the scatter plot and two for the diagonal plots.

By reviewing the annotated source code in this section, you should have a good start toward building a drill-down application from scratch. The full program listing for PLTSCATPLTHTML.SAS is also available in the SAS Online Samples, and you can run the application by opening UTMatrix.HTML in the HTMLBaseball subdirectory at the same location.

See Also

The QUIT statement is briefly reviewed in Section 2.5.

More Information

See Chapter 5, *"Bringing SAS/GRAPH Output to the Web,"* in *SAS/GRAPH Software Reference, Version 8*. Sections particularly helpful are
- Specifying Output Locations for HTML and GIF Files.
- Using the Output Delivery System (ODS) with SAS/GRAPH Software.
- About Drill-down Graphs. Especially helpful are the examples with bar chart links to three pie charts.

5.2.2 Enlarging the mouse plots

Figures 5.2.2a – 5.2.2c show how a Web application with ODS can be used to enlarge the 32 mouse tumor plots found in two separate 16-plot graphs. Links constructed in ANNOTATE data sets enable the user to go back and forth between the two graphs:

```
data anno1;
  length html text $30 function style color $8
  retain xsys ysys '3';
  function='symbol'; style='none'; color='blue';
    text='dot'; size=2; x=60; y=97;
    html='href="Last16.html"'; output;   ❶
  function='Label'; color='black'; style='swiss';
    size=1.25; x=62; y=97; position='6';
    text='Blue DOT For Last 16 Mice'; html=' '; output;   ❷ ❸
  stop;
run;
```

❶   The HTML variable defines a link from FIRST16.HTML to LAST16.HTML.

❷   Prompting text for the user.

❸   The HTML variable is set to missing so that only the DOT and not the prompting text becomes a hot spot in FIRST16.GIF.

ANNO1 above is attached to PROC GSLIDE that serves as a grand title in FIRST16.HTML that displays the first 16 mouse plots. Clicking on a data point in any of the small plots brings up an enlarged version of four plots in the same row.

PLOT32HTML.SAS can be found in the SAS Online Samples, and you can run the application by opening FIRST16.HTML in the HTMLMice subdirectory at the same location.

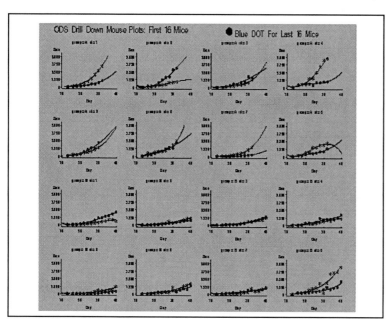

Figure 5.2.2a   *Clicking the blue dot takes the viewer to the second page of 16 plots.*

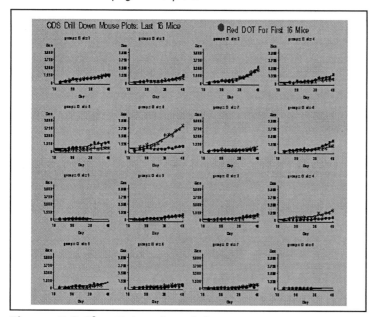

Figure 5.2.2b   *Clicking the red dot returns the viewer to the first page of 16 plots. Pressing any point on the graph drills down to an enlargement of the corresponding row of four plots.*

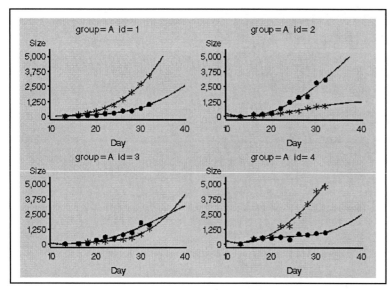

Figure 5.2.2c   *Clicking a point on A2 in Figure 5.2.2a brings up an enlargement of the first row of plots. Visual thinning has been eliminated to improve the readability of the enlarged graphs. All axes are fully rendered.*

The coverage of drill-down Web applications for plot enlargements rounds out the discussion about multiple-plot displays. One of the major themes in this book has been the need to rework a multiple-plot graphics project until a quality product is produced. The GREPLAY extension macros make the revisions easier, and data thinning enables important information to be communicated more economically to the viewer. Sometimes, however, nothing can replace a detailed view of the data. Drill-down provides a viable alternative because the detailed view is presented in conjunction with the larger picture.

More Information

For a description of how the HTML variable is used in an ANNOTATE data set, see Chapter 11, "Annotate Dictionary," *SAS/GRAPH Software Reference, Version 8, Volume 1*, pp. 462–63.

References

SAS Institute Documentation

SAS Institute Inc. 1991. *SAS/GRAPH Software: Reference, Version 6.* 1st ed. 2 vols. Cary, NC: SAS Institute Inc.

SAS Institute Inc. 1999. *SAS/GRAPH Software: Reference, Version 8.* 2 vols. Cary, NC: SAS Institute Inc.

SAS Institute Inc. 1991. *SAS/GRAPH Software: Usage, Version 6.* 1st ed. Cary, NC: SAS Institute Inc.

SAS Institute Inc. 1991. *SAS/STAT User's Guide, Version 8.* 3 vols. Cary, NC: SAS Institute Inc.

Articles, Papers, and Books

Brown, L. M. 1991. "Using the VBAR and HBAR Statements and the TEMPLATE Facility to Create Side-by-Side, Horizontal Bar Charts with Shared Vertical Axes Labels." *Proceedings of the Sixteenth Annual SAS Users Group International Conference,* New Orleans, LA, 750–54.

Carpenter, A. 1998. *Carpenter's Complete Guide to the SAS Macro Language.* Cary, NC: SAS Institute Inc.

Carpenter, A. 1999. *Annotate: Simply the Basics.* Cary, NC: SAS Institute Inc.

Carpenter, A. L., and C. E. Shipp. 1995. *Quick Results with SAS/GRAPH Software.* Cary, NC: SAS Institute Inc.

Corning, B. 1994. "Input/Output." *Observations* 3 (4): 69–70.

Easter, G., and C. Noto. 1995. "Input/Output." *Observations* 4 (4): 55–57.

Elkin, S. E. 1987. "Organizing Your SAS Graphs." *Proceedings of the Twenty-Third Annual SAS Users Group International Conference,* Nashville, TN, 505–6.

Friendly, M. 1991. *SAS System for Statistical Graphics.* 1st ed. Cary, NC: SAS Institute Inc.

Friendly, M. 2000. *Visualizing Categorical Data.* Cary, NC: SAS Institute Inc.

Gaccione, P. 1996. "Multiple Plots Per Page? Graphics and Template Catalogs Make It Easy," *Proceedings of the Twenty-First Annual SAS Users Group International Conference.* Chicago, 943–48.

Gilbert, J. D. 2000. "Replaying Graphics with PROC GREPLAY." *Proceedings of the Twenty-Fifth Annual SAS Users Group International Conference,* Indianapolis, IN, 165–25.

Jacobs, M. 1993. "An Introduction to PROC GREPLAY." *Proceedings of the Eighteenth Annual SAS Users Group International Conference, New York,* 1366–72.

Kalbfleisch, J. D., and R. L. Prentice. 1980. *The Statistical Analysis of Failure Time Data.* New York: Wiley.

Kalt, M. 1986. "Creative Uses of PROC GREPLAY." *Proceedings of the Twenty-Fifth Annual SAS Users Group International Conference,* Indianapolis, IN, 165–25.

Kalt, M. 1993. "Input/Output." *Observations* 2 (4): 62–64.

Kirk, G. F., and A. Horney. 1998. "Exploring Multi-dimensional Relationships with SAS/GRAPH Software." *Proceedings of the Twenty-Third Annual SAS Users Group International Conference,* Nashville, TN, 1100–1106.

Leighton, R. W. 1994. "Working with Arrays: Doing More with Less Code." *Proceedings of the Nineteenth Annual SAS Users Group International Conference,* Dallas, TX, 1314–24.

McFadden, F., and J. A. Hoffer. 1994. *Modern Database Management,* 4th ed. Redwood City, CA: Benjamin Cummings.

Miron, T. 1995. *The How-To Book for SAS/GRAPH Software.* Cary, NC: SAS Institute Inc.

Mitchell, K. A., et al. 1992. "The Greplay Procedure: A Valuable Tool for the SAS Graphics User." *Proceedings of the Seventeenth Annual SAS Users Group International Conference,* Honolulu, HI, 1209–13.

Noto, C., and M. Kalt. "Dynamically Creating Templates with PROC GREPLAY." *Observations,* October 12, 1997. Available http://www.sas.com/service/library/periodicals/obs/obswww04/index.html.

Redman, J. 1991. "Input/Output." *Observations* 1 (1): 59–61.

Redman, J. 1993. "Input/Output." in *Observations* 2 (3): 58–60.

Rooth, N. P. 1987. "PROC GREPLAY: Developing a Presentation That Your Users Will Appreciate." *Proceedings of the Twelfth Annual SAS Users Group International Conference*, Dallas, TX, 168–74.

Shoemaker, J. 1998. "Advanced Techniques to Build and Manage User-Defined SAS FORMAT Catalogs." *Proceedings of the Eleventh Annual Northeast SAS Users Group Conference*, Pittsburgh, PA, 102–7.

Shoemaker, J. 2000. "Ten Things You Should Know about PROC FORMAT." *Proceedings of the Thirteenth Annual Northeast SAS Users Group Conference*, Philadelphia, PA, 242–46.

Thome-Polingo, L. 1993. "Is It Possible to Print More Than One Graph on a Page? A Comparison of PROC GREPLAY and the DATA Step Graphics Interface DSGI." *Proceedings of the Eighteenth Annual SAS Users Group International Conference*, New York, 1475–80.

Tufte, E. R. 1983. *The Visual Display of Quantitative Information.* Cheshire, CT: Graphics Press.

Tukey, J. W. 1977. *Exploratory Data Analysis.* Reading, MA: Addison Wesley.

Tukey, P. A., and J. W. Tukey. 1981. "Data-Driven View Selection; Agglomeration and Sharpening." In *Interpreting Multivariate Data,* ed. Vic Barnett, 231-32. Chichester, UK: Wiley.

Vierkant, R. A. 1998. "Creating Scatterplot Matrices Using SAS/GRAPH Software." *Proceedings of the Twenty-Fifth Annual SAS Users Group International Conference*, Indianapolis, IN, 821–26.

Watts, P. 1997. "Tips for Producing Customized Graphs with SAS/GRAPH Software." *Proceedings of the Tenth Annual Northeast SAS Users Group Conference*, Baltimore, MD, 497–505.

Watts, P. 1998. "Managing SAS/GRAPH Displays with the GREPLAY Procedure." *Proceedings of the Eleventh Annual Northeast SAS Users Group Conference*, Pittsburgh, PA, 439–45.

Watts, P. 2001. "Defining Colors with Precision in Your SAS/GRAPH Application." *Proceedings of the Fourteenth Annual Northeast SAS Users Group Conference*, Baltimore, MD, 347–48.

Watts, P. 2001. "The Relationship between Format Structure and Efficiency in SAS." *Proceedings of the Fourteenth Annual Northeast SAS Users Group Conference*, Baltimore, MD, 697–705.

Watts, P., and S. Litwin. 1991. "Using SAS/GRAPH Software to Create Trees That Model Developmental Biological Phenomena." *Proceedings of the Sixteenth Annual SAS Users Group International Conference,* New Orleans, LA, 779–84.

Watts, P., and S. Litwin. 1992. "Using SAS/GRAPH Software for Three-Dimensional Illustrations of Amino Acid Diversity." *Proceedings of the Seventeenth Annual SAS Users Group International Conference,* Honolulu, HI, 1249–54.

Westerlund, E. R. 1999. "%manyplot: A Macro for Plotting Many Graphs on a Single Page." *Proceedings of the Twelfth Annual Northeast SAS Users Group Conference,* Washington, DC, 352–53.

Yourdon, E., et al. 1995. *Mainstream Objects: An Analysis and Design Approach for Business.* Upper Saddle River, NJ: Prentice Hall.

Appendix : Enlarged Graphs and Extension Macro Source Code

Selected full-sized graphs are included in this Appendix for better viewing. In addition, all extension macros except %DELGCAT are listed in their entirety. A complete listing of the DELGCAT macro can be found on page 33 in Chapter 3, "The Macros."

Additional two-strata survival plots from the VA lung cancer data

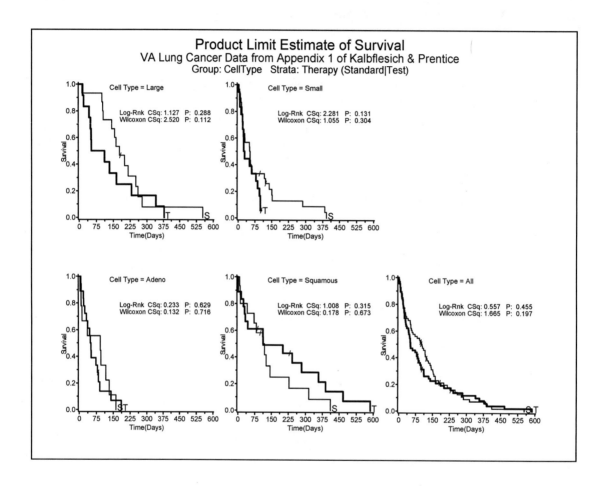

Additional two-strata survival plots from the VA lung cancer data

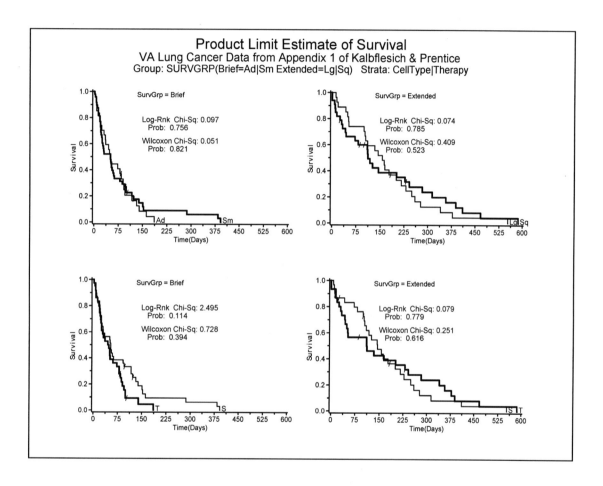

Complete display of the mouse tumor data

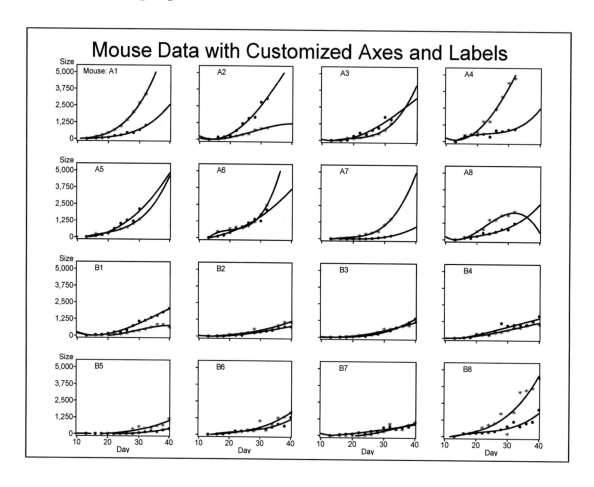

Complete display of the mouse tumor data

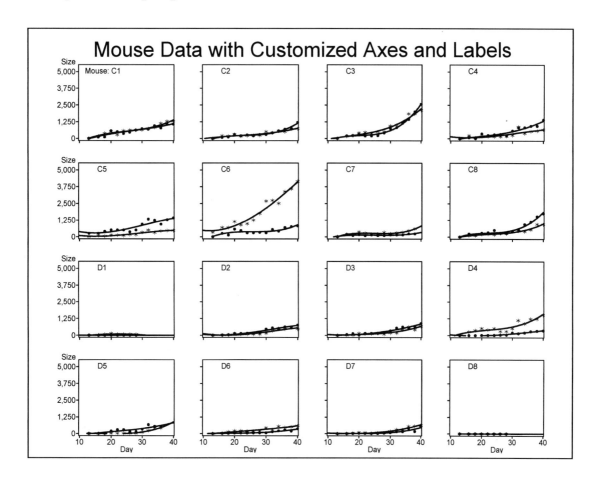

Enlarged graph of the Shannon Scores for amino acid diversity

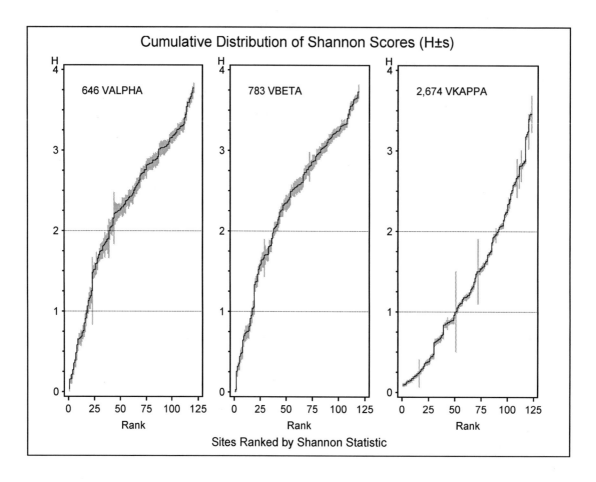

Schematic graph for 3-D plots that uses another method to deal with text and shape distortion

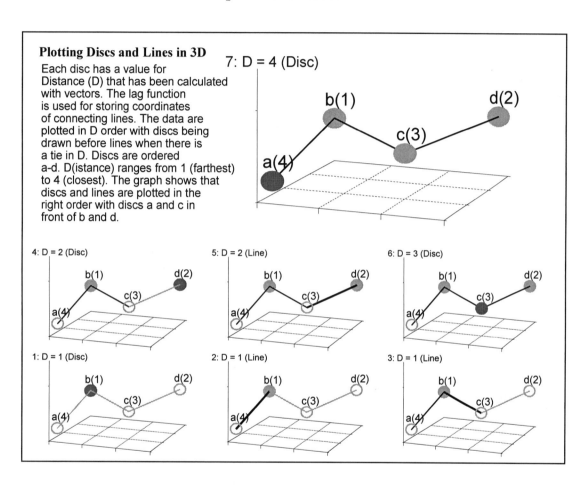

Plotting Discs and Lines in 3D

Each disc has a value for Distance (D) that has been calculated with vectors. The lag function is used for storing coordinates of connecting lines. The data are plotted in D order with discs being drawn before lines when there is a tie in D. Discs are ordered a-d. D(istance) ranges from 1 (farthest) to 4 (closest). The graph shows that discs and lines are plotted in the right order with discs a and c in front of b and d.

7: D = 4 (Disc)

b(1)   d(2)   c(3)   a(4)

4: D = 2 (Disc)   5: D = 2 (Line)   6: D = 3 (Disc)

1: D = 1 (Disc)   2: D = 1 (Line)   3: D = 1 (Line)

Complete display of the upper triangular scatterplot matrix of baseball data

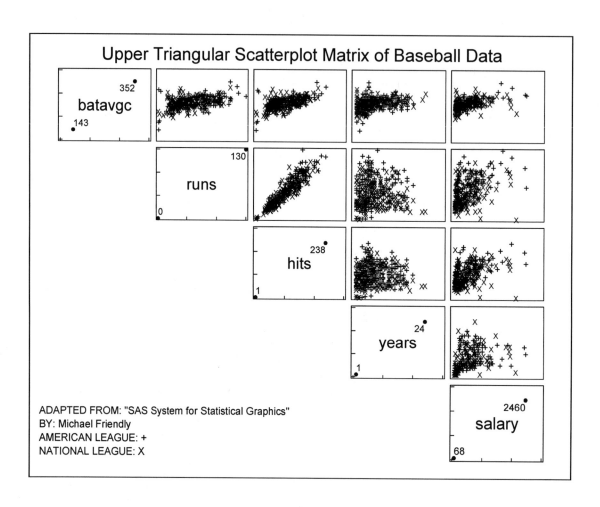

TMPLT macro for building a template with PROC GREPLAY

```
/*   -------------------------------------------------------------------
     Program  :  Tmplt.sas

     Project  :  Multiple-Plot Displays: Simplified with Macros
     Path     :  Your SASAUTOS folder

     Purpose  :  Generate a template for multiple plot displays. Optionally
                 invoke the nested macro %TREPLAY to replay plots from the
                 designated graphics catalog lockstep through the newly
                 generated panels.

     Input    :  Values for macro parameters

     Output   :  A template catalog entry

     Params   :  For a full description see page 37 in Chapter 3.
                 MARGIN   space surrounding the group of small panels on a page
                 SCALEX   Scale factor along the X-axis
                 SCALEY   Scale factor along the Y-axis
                 XLATEX   Translate or move panels along the X-axis
                 XLATEY   Translate or move panels along the Y-axis
                 R1...R8  Number of panels in Row1 to Row8 (max 8 rows)
                 COLOR    Color=border-color
                 ROTATE   Rotate=degrees
                 CLIP     Clip graphics at panel boundaries
                 IGOUT    Name of the graphics catalog
                 TC       Name of output template catalog
                 TNAME    Template name
                 TREPLAY  A switch for invoking the nested %TREPLAY macro

     Usage    :  How to work with TREPLAY internally as %TREPLAY and in
                    open code for customized applications:
                 *Default layout for 6 out of 6 plots in a 4-panel display:
                   Page 1:
                   /*/ /*/
                   /*/ /*/
                   Page 2:
                   /*/ /*/
                   / / / / (blank)
                 Macro Invocation:
                   %TMPLT(R1=2, R2=2, TREPLAY=Y);

                 *Default layout for 6 out of 6 plots in a 3-panel display:
                   Page 1:
                   /*/ /*/
                     /*/
                   Page 2:
                   /*/ /*/
                     /*/
                 Macro Invocation:
                   %TMPLT(R1=2, R2=1, TREPLAY=Y);

                 *Customized layout for plots #4, 2,and 1 out of 6 plots
                  in a 3-panel display:
                   Page 1 (only):
```

```
       /*/ /*/
        /*/
Macro Invocation:
   %TMPLT(R1=2, R2=1, TREPLAY=N);
   treplay(1:4 2:2 3:1);

*Customized layout right-justified 3 out of 3 plots in a
4-panel display.
   /*/ /*/
   / / /*/
Macro Invocation:
   %TMPLT(R1=2, R2=2, TREPLAY=N);
   treplay(1:1 2:2 4:3);
```

-- */

TREPLAY macro nested within the TMPLT macro

```
%macro Tmplt(Margin=0,ScaleX=1,ScaleY=1,XLateX=0,XLateY=0,
             R1= ,R2= ,R3= ,R4= ,R5= ,R6= ,R7= ,R8= ,
             color=NONE,rotate=0,clip=OFF,
             igout=work.gseg,tc=tempcat,tname=TmpMac,Treplay=N);

/* **************
   treplay uses macro variables IGOUT and NPANELS from %tmplt
   *********** */
%macro treplay;

/*-- Obtain number of plots */
 %let indexL=%eval(%index(&igout,.)-1);
 %let indexM=%eval(&indexL.+2);
 %let libname=%upcase(%substr(&igout,1,&indexL));
 %let memname=%upcase(%substr(&igout,&indexM));

 proc sql noprint;
    select left(trim(put(count(*),2.))) into :nplots
    from dictionary.catalogs
    where upcase(libname) eq "&libname"
      and upcase(memname) eq "&memname"
      and substr(objname,1,1) eq 'G';
 quit;

/*-- write the TREPLAY command */
 proc greplay nofs igout=&igout tc=&tc;
 Template &tname;

%let numgrafs=%sysfunc(ceil(&nplots./&npanels.) );
%let plot=1;
%do i= 1 %to &numgrafs;
    treplay
      %do panel=1 %to &npanels;

       /*-- Last panel is always the grand title GSLIDE */
         %if &panel eq &npanels %then %do;
            &panel.:&nplots.
         %end;
```

```
                  /*-- puts all non grand-title plots on a graph.*/
                  %else %if &plot lt &nplots %then %do;
                     &panel.:&plot.
                     %let plot=%eval(&plot + 1);
                  %end;
            %end;
         ; %*-- terminating semicolon for Treplay;
      %end;
      run;
      %mend treplay

/*-- Back to Tmplt*

/* **************
   calculate Macro Variables:
   MARGIN2 for border allotment around the small plots
   MAXNCOL is the maximum Number of plots in a row of plots
   NROWS   is the total number of rows in a graph
   NPANELS is the sum of N1 ... N8
   *********** */
%let margin2 = %sysevalf(2.0 * &margin);
%let MaxNCol= 0;
%let NRows= 0;
%let NPanels=0;
%do i=1 %to 8;
   %if &&r&i ne %then %do;
      %let NROWS = &i;
      %if &&r&i gt &MaxNCol %then %let maxncol=&&r&i;
      %let NPanels = %eval(&NPanels + &&r&i);
   %end;
%end;
%let Npanels = %eval(&NPANELS +1);    %*--for grand title

proc greplay tc=&tc igout=&igout nofs

   tdef &TName
   /*-- Correct parameter errors */
%if %sysevalf(&ScaleX gt 1.0,boolean) %then %do;
   %put ==>Maximum ScaleX factor is 1.0;
   %let ScaleX=1.0;
%end;
%if %sysevalf(&ScaleY gt 1.0,boolean) %then %do;
   %put ==>Maximum ScaleY factor is 1.0;
   %let ScaleY=1.0;
%end;

/*-- Want XLates to be within the bounds of the margin */
/*-- X */
%if %sysevalf(%sysevalf(-1.0 * &XLateX) gt &Margin , boolean) %then %do;
   %put ==>Maximum Abs(XLateX) is the Margin: &margin;
   %let XLateX = %sysevalf(-1.0 * &Margin );
%end;
%if %sysevalf(&XLateX gt &Margin , boolean) %then %do;
   %put ==>Maximum XLateX is the Margin: &margin;
   %let XLateX = %sysevalf(&Margin );
   %end;
```

```
/*-- Y */
%if %sysevalf(%sysevalf(-1.0 * &XLateY) gt &Margin , boolean) %then %do;
    %put ==>Maximum Abs(XLateY) is the Margin: &Margin;
    %let XLateY = %sysevalf(-1.0 * &Margin );
%end;
%if %sysevalf(&XLateY gt &Margin, boolean) %then %do;
    %put ==>Maximum XLateY is the Margin: &margin;
    %let XLateY = %sysevalf(&Margin );
%end

%if %sysevalf(&NRows gt 8, boolean)  %then %do;
    %put Maximum Number of Rows of panels is 8;
    %let NRows=8;
%end

/*-- Calculate panel coordinates *

/* ***************
    Height and width are calculated for the individual panels.
    The width of each panel is determined by the row containing
    the greatest number of panels. (MAXNCOL)
    *********** */
%let height=%sysevalf((100-&Margin2.)/&NRows);
%let width=%sysevalf((100-&Margin2.)/&MaxNCol)

%let PanelNum=1;
%do row = 1 %to &NRows;            %*-- for Y coordinates;
    %do column = 1 %to &&R&row;    %*-- for X coordinates;
    /* ***************
        Calculate Y coordinates top to bottom. This makes y1
        greater in value than y2.Calc y1, y2 ONCE per row of
        panels (when &column=1).
        *********** */
    %if &column eq 1 %then %do;
        %if &row eq 1 %then %do;   %*--row1,col1=panel1 upper left;
          %let y1=%sysevalf(100.0-(&margin ));
        %end;
        %else %do;
          %let y1 = &y2;
%*-- following rows: relative calculation;
        %end;
        %let y2=%sysevalf(&y1-&height);
    %end; %*-- calculating Y coords;

    /* ***************
        Calculate X Coordinates. The number of columns (panels per row)
        can be different. Templates are always centered like this
                |--||--||--|  (3 panels)
                 |--||--|   (2 panels)
        Therefore, get coords for 1st template to the far left by
        calculating from the middle (50%). Width allows for margin.
        *********** */

    %if &column=1 %then %do;
```

```
      %let x1 = %sysevalf(50-(&&R&row./2 * &width));
    %end;
    %else %do;
      %let x1=&x2;       %*-- next col left-X = current col right-X;
    %end;
    %let x2=%sysevalf(&x1+&width)

    /* -- write out a panel */
    &PanelNum / llx=&x1 ulx=&x1 urx=&x2 lrx=&x2
                lly=&y2 uly=&y1 ury=&y1 lry=&y2
                ScaleX=&ScaleX ScaleY=&ScaleY
                XLateX=&XLateX XLateY=&XLateY
                Rotate=&Rotate
                %if %upcase(&color) ne NONE %then Color=&Color;
                %if %upcase(&clip) ne OFF %then %str(clip)

    %let PanelNum=%eval(&PanelNum+1)

  %end;   %*-- column;
%end;     %*-- row

  /*-- For the Grand Title */
  &PanelNum / llx=0 ulx=0 urx=100 lrx=100
            lly=0 uly=100 ury=100 lry=0

  /*-- Assign template */
  Template &TName

run;

  /*-- Conditionally invoke %Treplay for lock-step panel|plot assignments */

%if %upcase(&treplay) eq Y %then %do;
    %treplay;
  %end;
%mend Tmplt;
```

SIZEIT macro for correcting text and shape distortion

```
/*   -------------------------------------------------------------------
     Program   :  SizeIt.sas

     Project   :  Multiple-Plot Displays: Simplified with Macros
     Path      :  Your SASAUTOS folder

     Purpose   :  Generates goption HSize and VSize lengths given
                  XMax and YMax from PROC GDEVICE. Use this macro to
                  correct Text and Shape distortion caused by oblong plots.

     Input     :  Values for macro parameters
     Output    :  GOPTIONS HSIZE and VSIZE statement that corrects distortion

     Params    :  For a full description see page 51 in Chapter 3.
              MARGIN   space surrounding the group of small panels on a page
              SCALEX   Scale factor along the X-axis
              SCALEY   Scale factor along the Y-axis
              NROWS    Number of rows containing plots
                       (Calculated in %TMPLT. Entered here.)
              MAXNCOL  Maximum number of plots in a row of plots
                       (Calculated in %TMPLT. Entered here.)
              XMAX     used for calculating HSIZE
              YMAX     used for calculating VSIZ

     Usage     :  Invocation values should be match those in %TMPLT for
                  MARGIN, SCALEX, and SCALEY. Calculated and entered values
                  should be the same for NROWS and MAXNCOL.
     ------------------------------------------------------------------- */
%macro SizeIt(Margin=0, ScaleX=1, ScaleY=1, NRows=, MaxNCol=, YMax=,
              XMax=)

%let margin2 = %sysevalf(2.0 * &margin); *-- for internal calculations;

*-- correct any param errors;
%if %sysevalf(&ScaleX gt 1.0,boolean) %then %do;
  %put Maximum ScaleX factor is 1.0;
  %let ScaleX=1.0;
%end;
%if %sysevalf(&ScaleY gt 1.0,boolean) %then %do;
  %put Maximum ScaleY factor is 1.0;
  %let ScaleY=1.0;
%end;
%if %sysevalf(&NRows gt 8, boolean)  %then %do;
  %put Maximum Number of Rows of panels is 8;
  %let NRows=8;
%end;

*-- Calculate VSIZE and HSIZE. ;
%let VSize=%sysevalf(((100-&Margin2)/&NRows) * &ScaleY * &YMax *0.01);
%let HSize=%sysevalf(((100-&Margin2)/&MaxNCol) * &ScaleX * &XMax *0.01);

*-- the output;
goptions vsize=&VSize in hsize=&HSize in;
%mend SizeIt;
```

```
*-- Calculate VSIZE and HSIZE. ;
%let VSize=%sysevalf(((100-&Margin2)/&NRows) * &ScaleY * &YMax *0.01);
%let HSize=%sysevalf(((100-&Margin2)/&MaxNCol) * &ScaleX * &XMax *0.01);

*-- the output;
goptions vsize=&VSize in hsize=&HSize in;
%mend SizeIt;
```

Index

Call your local SAS office to order these books from Books by Users Press

Annotate: Simply the Basics
by **Art Carpenter** . . . . .Order No. A57320

Applied Multivariate Statistics with SAS® Software,
Second Edition
by **Ravindra Khattree**
and **Dayanand N. Naik** . . . . .Order No. A56903

Applied Statistics and the SAS® Programming
Language, Fourth Edition
by **Ronald P. Cody**
and **Jeffrey K. Smith** . . . . .Order No. A55984

An Array of Challenges — Test Your SAS® Skills
by **Robert Virgile** . . . . .Order No. A55625

Beyond the Obvious with SAS® Screen Control
Language
by **Don Stanley** . . . . .Order No. A55073

Carpenter's Complete Guide to the SAS® Macro
Language
by **Art Carpenter** . . . . .Order No. A56100

The Cartoon Guide to Statistics
by **Larry Gonick**
and **Woollcott Smith** . . . . .Order No. A55153

Categorical Data Analysis Using the SAS® System,
Second Edition
by **Maura E. Stokes, Charles S. Davis,**
and **Gary G. Koch** . . . . .Order No. A57998

Client/Server Survival Guide, Third Edition
by **Robert Orfali, Dan Harkey,**
and **Jeri Edwards** . . . . .Order No. A58099

Cody's Data Cleaning Techniques Using SAS® Software
by **Ron Cody** . . . . .Order No. A57198

Common Statistical Methods for Clinical Research
with SAS® Examples, Second Edition
by **Glenn A. Walker** . . . . .Order No. A58086

Concepts and Case Studies in Data Management
by **William S. Calvert**
and **J. Meimei Ma** . . . . .Order No. A55220

Debugging SAS® Programs: A Handbook of Tools
and Techniques
by **Michele M. Burlew** . . . . .Order No. A57743

Efficiency: Improving the Performance of Your SAS®
Applications
by **Robert Virgile** . . . . .Order No. A55960

Extending SAS® Survival Analysis Techniques for
Medical Research
by **Alan Cantor** . . . . .Order No. A55504

A Handbook of Statistical Analyses Using SAS®,
Second Edition
by **B.S. Everitt**
and **G. Der** . . . . .Order No. A58679

Health Care Data and the SAS® System
by **Marge Scerbo, Craig Dickstein,**
and **Alan Wilson** . . . . .Order No. A57638

The How-To Book for SAS/GRAPH® Software
by **Thomas Miron** . . . . .Order No. A55203

Working with the SAS® System
by **Erik W. Tilanus** . . . . .Order No. A55190

*Your Guide to Survey Research Using the
SAS® System*
by **Archer Gravely** . . . . .Order No. A55688

JMP® Books

Basic Business Statistics: A Casebook
by **Dean P. Foster, Robert A. Stine,**
and **Richard P. Waterman** . . . . .Order No. A56813

Business Analysis Using Regression: A Casebook
by **Dean P. Foster, Robert A. Stine,**
and **Richard P. Waterman** . . . . .Order No. A56818

JMP® Start Statistics, Second Edition
by **John Sall, Ann Lehman,**
and **Lee Creighton** . . . . .Order No. A58166

*Welcome * Bienvenue * Willkommen * Yohkoso * Bienvenido*

SAS Publishing Is Easy to Reach

Visit our Web page located at www.sas.com/pubs

You will find product and service details, including

- **sample chapters**
- **tables of contents**
- **author biographies**
- **book reviews**

Learn about

- **regional user groups conferences**
- **trade show sites and dates**
- **authoring opportunities**
- **custom textbooks**

Explore all the services that Publications has to offer!

Your Listserv Subscription Automatically Brings the News to You

Do you want to be among the first to learn about the latest books and services available from SAS Publishing? Subscribe to our listserv **newdocnews-l** and, once each month, you will automatically receive a description of the newest books and which environments or operating systems and SAS® release(s) each book addresses.

To subscribe,

1. Send an e-mail message to **listserv@vm.sas.com**

2. Leave the "Subject" line blank

3. Use the following text for your message:

subscribe **NEWDOCNEWS-L** *your-first-name your-last-name*

For example: subscribe NEWDOCNEWS-L John Doe

Create Customized Textbooks Quickly, Easily, and Affordably

SelecText® offers instructors at U.S. colleges and universities a way to create custom textbooks for courses that teach students how to use SAS software.

For more information, see our Web page at **www.sas.com/selectext**, or contact our SelecText coordinators by sending e-mail to **selectext@sas.com**.

You're Invited to Publish with SAS Institute's Books by Users Program

If you enjoy writing about SAS software and how to use it, the Books by Users Program at SAS Institute offers a variety of publishing options. We are actively recruiting authors to publish books and sample code. Do you find the idea of writing a book by yourself a little intimidating? Consider writing with a co-author. Keep in mind that you will receive complete editorial and publishing support, access to our users, technical advice and assistance, and competitive royalties. Please contact us for an author packet. E-mail us at **sasbbu@sas.com** or call 919-531-7447. See the Books by Users Web page at **www.sas.com/bbu** for complete information.

Book Discount Offered at SAS Public Training Courses!

When you attend one of our SAS Public Training Courses at any of our regional Training Centers in the U.S., you will receive a 20% discount on any book orders placed during the course. Take advantage of this offer at the next course you attend!

SAS Institute Inc.
SAS Campus Drive
Cary, NC 27513-2414
Fax 919-677-4444

E-mail: sasbook@sas.com
Web page: www.sas.com/pubs
To order books, call Fulfillment Services at 800-727-3228*
For other SAS Institute business, call 919-677-8000*

* Note: Customers outside the U.S. should contact their local SAS office.

The Power to Know.™

SAS Publishing